Retirement Is for the Birds

by

Jocelyn Reichel

Illustrated by
Martha Reichel Hekman

MOODY PRESS
CHICAGO

Library of Congress Cataloging in Publication Data

Reichel, Jocelyn.
    Retirement is for the birds.

    1. Retirement. I. Title.
HQ1062.R36   646.7'9   81-18982
ISBN 0-8024-7295-8   AACR2

Moody Press, a ministry of the Moody Bible Institute, is designed for education, evangelization, and edification.

Printed in the United States of America

Contents

By Way Of Introduction . . .

THERE IS A TINY SHELTERED COVE in the wilderness park a few miles from our home where we go of a summer afternoon with our Chihuahua, Poquito, and our transistor radio. We spread a blanket on the warm sand and eat a picnic lunch while we listen to the Cubs, three hundred miles south of us in Wrigley Field, play ball. Sometimes we just lie in the healing sun and read. Or watch the waves breaking on the shore and think long thoughts. We have found it a good place to feed our souls, to count our blessings, to make decisions.

It was for that last reason that we were there on a Saturday in September several years ago. Not that we had any discussing to do; we had already spent two years in debate. Nor did we intend to review our pros and cons. We knew them by heart. We were there so I could make a pronouncement.

But I was in no hurry, content to lie quietly, letting my mind unclench and my spirit expand; distracted for a few happy moments watching our aging Poquito race around like a puppy, led on by the odors of rabbit and chipmunk wafted on the breeze. Frantically darting, whuffing, and panting from burrow to burrow, diving into the excavations as far as her girth would permit, backing out and shaking the redolent earth from her ears, she finally dashed over to share her ecstasy with us for a brief second. Lucky dog, untroubled by decision-making!

Decisions are always difficult for me; big ones, that is. I can cope with questions like "Soup or salad?" or "Wash or dry?" My little decisions are snap ones and rarely cause me second thoughts. However, I take a prodigious amount of time over the momentous moves. I make innumerable lists of "Why I Shoulds" and "Why I Shouldn'ts." I worry my husband and my offspring with repeated discussions of the problem at hand. I lie awake night after night in fretful self-analysis, fearful that I might eventually make up my mind for all the wrong reasons.

I oscillate between "Yes, I will!" and "No, I won't!" a hundred times a day. Finally exasperated, I reach the end of myself, and I settle down to talk it over with the Proper Authority, acknowledging that whatever decision I make needs only one criterion: it must be the Lord's will for me.

But even my prayers tend to be neurotic. I ask for signs. Definite signs. "Open a door before me, Lord," I ask, "and when You do, let the hinges squeak." "Shut the door behind me," I plead, "and shut it quickly and with a loud slam." I don't want to miss my cues. I want to be sure.

Especially this time I wanted to be sure. For two years I had been wrestling with a heavy decision — whether or not to resign from my position in a Chicago high school, a career into which the Lord had led me twenty-one years before. He had not only called me into teaching, He had seen me through three-and-a-half years of frenetic juggling of college and family responsibilities. He had placed me in convenient and congenial schools during most of my career; walked me through a Master's degree plus thirty-six additional graduate hours so that I was now at top salary and

6

secure tenure. No wonder my growing dissatisfaction with my job was accompanied by the conviction that I was guilty of crass ingratitude, and that I should be thoroughly ashamed of myself.

Not only was I carrying a load of guilt, I was encountering a few hurdles. For one thing, I was uncertain as to the purity of my motives. A few years earlier, we had bought a vacation and retirement home in rural Wisconsin; a hideaway to which we fled every weekend. How could I be positive that my desire to resign was not merely a selfish craving for a lazy, slow-paced, close-to-nature existence? A middle-aged cop-out? I couldn't. Not without a lot of soul searching and prayer.

Then, too, my husband had taken an early retirement. Did I resent it that he could spend weeks at a time in the country while I worked my sixteen-hour-a-day, five-days-a-week, 200-pupil job? I knew I did. And the only way I could see around that resentment to find out the Lord's will — forget about MY want — was through prayer.

A move like the one we were contemplating had to be well prayed out. It would mean a drastic change in life-style — from urban to rural, and more importantly, from financial freestyle to frugality. Following the advice of a beloved and popular Chicago radio pastor, I prayed that if the Lord wanted me to remain in teaching, He would rekindle my enthusiasm and restore my zest for my work; and that if He wanted me to leave, He would make it intolerable for me to stay.

I got my answer. During my two years of importunity, my job became more and more distasteful. My blood pressure resisted treatment and continued to rise; I functioned almost continually in a "stroke zone." Insomnia became a real problem, and chronic depression crept in. Stress and hypertension led to gastrointestinal difficulties. I was the epitome of "Teacher Burnout." It took me two years to recognize that I was burning out — to acknowledge that the Lord was giving me my answer.

So here we were that Saturday in September of '77, basking at "Inspiration Cove." In three days I was due back in the classroom for fall semester, having spent the entire summer under a perpetual overcast. I sat up abruptly, brushed the sand from my hands and announced without preamble, "I'm going to resign."

"Good!" Everett responded. I heard relief and satisfaction and congratulation in that one word.

"I'll return on Tuesday and notify the principal that I'll be leaving in January. That will give me one last semester to get my senior division records in order, to get all my classes off to a solid start — and it will give us plenty of time to dispose of our furniture and vacate our apartment." There was a tremor in my voice, but it was of excitement, not fear.

It's a strange and wondrous thing that happens when one chooses rightly. A boulder rolled from my back. A tightness left my chest. And I *knew* that the Lord had been waiting for me to take this step.

In the ensuing five months, as I tied up loose ends at school and at home and made preparations to leave Chicago permanently, I had no second thoughts, only a recurring refrain "Thank You, Lord! Thank You!" that I couldn't have restrained if I had wanted to.

By now we have been country folk for more than four years. The following is our journalized account of the flavor and texture of life "away from it all."

1

Retirement Is for the Birds!

EVERETT AND I HAVE A DECISION TO MAKE. It's time to consider our alternatives. The slab of suet in the freezer is dwindling fast, and the fifty-pound bag of sunflower seeds out in the barn is nearly empty. The birds in our backyard have recognized for some time what my husband and I are reluctant to admit — winter is on the way.

Black-capped chickadees, infrequent snackers during the summer, are now industriously flitting back and forth, gorging from sunrise to sunset. The purple finches have returned en masse and more or less amicably share the feeders with the chickadees; bluejays swooping down out of the branches above scatter the lot of them; nuthatches hang nervously around the fringes, downside up.

Now, I tell Everett. *Now,* before the invasion of the evening grosbeaks, we must decide whether we are going to close down our backyard cafeteria for the winter — and thus remain financially solvent — or continue feeding our feathered freeloaders and risk having to negotiate a bank loan. It is an old debate that we renew with vigor every autumn.

It has not always been thus. Before we escaped to rural Wisconsin, we were city slickers. Mention bird feeders to us, and chances are we would have conjured up childhood memories of glass-globed, peanut-filled vending machines installed at every Chicago elevated station. Put a penny in the slot and Voilà! a hundred hungry pigeons would descend from the rafters to perch chummily on our shoulders and eat trustingly from our palms. A few pennies now and then, a few slices of stale bread at the lakefront parks, and we were in tune with St. Francis of Assisi!

But then we forsook city living to rusticate in the woods, and one of our daughters, worried that what we had in mind was not retiring but vegetating, gave us a bird-feeder as a house-warming present — an attempt to keep the old folks entertained and alert and out of the rocking chair. Along with the feeder, she presented us with a two-pound sack of wild bird seed. "To get you started," she said. What she got us started on was an expensive hobby that may eventually send my retired husband back to work or both of us to debtor's prison!

Remember the movie *Mary Poppins*? Remember the scene in which Mary encouraged, "Feed the birds. Feed the birds. Tuppence a bag"? Mary even promised, "You won't be sorry!" Well, she was not singing about your ordinary backyard daily visitors, like bluejays and sparrows. She had in mind a flock of psittacosic pigeons pirouetting on the steps of St. Paul's Cathedral, panhandling tourists. That kind of charity we find no quarrel with. It's the benevolence that begins at home, right on our own doorstep, that hurts.

Now, Wisconsin natives are aware that one doesn't have to work overtime in the summer to attract a few birds; just shaking out the tablecloth over the porch railing after supper will do the trick. But we were cheechakos from Chicago. So in June when the chickadees, nuthatches, and rose-breasted grosbeaks accepted our invitation to dine, we were patheti-

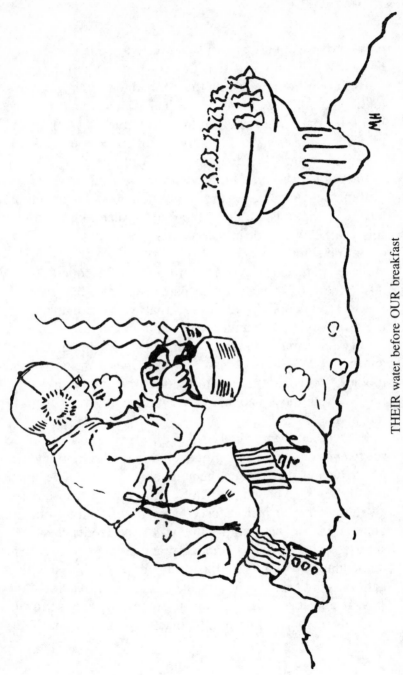

THEIR water before OUR breakfast

cally and awesomely grateful. We were a shade less exuberant when cowbirds and starlings crashed the party.

By July we were boasting that we had to switch from two- to five-pound bags of seed; we had added oranges to the menu for the orioles and catbirds, and cracked corn for the mourning doves. We jokingly rationalized our extravagances, saying: "We don't smoke, drink, or chew."

In August we knew for certain that we had cornered the bird market when we overheard our neighbors commenting, "How strange! There don't seem to be many birds around this year!" Well, not in *their* yards, anyway.

Before summer's end we had an aviary worth envying — and we were carting home birdseed in 25-pound sacks. Also, the local butcher, who had been providing us with free suet, had convinced himself that we were manufacturing explosives or laundry soap and began to charge us twenty-five cents a pound. "Oh well," we reminded one another. "We don't smoke, drink, chew, or go to the movies," closing our eyes to the fact that although we did not cultivate those habits, neither did we allow for them in our budget.

In October Everett had to buy an air rifle to discourage the twenty or so voracious squirrels who had moved into the territory, and also to keep the neighbors' cats from decimating our flocks. I called the rifle a "sting ray" because that's all the potency it had at forty feet — the distance from the gun turret, our bathroom window, to the feeder area. My spouse, who had received commendation for excellent marksmanship while in the army, enjoyed his shooting gallery — until the day he concussed a starling that got in the way of a beebee intended for the rump of a gray squirrel.

Cold weather set in, and the blackbirds and starlings left

12

with obvious reluctance. With the shortening of the days, more birds deserted the camp, and although we were sorry to see them leave, we looked forward to a winter respite — for ourselves and our checkbook. We took heart after a nearly birdless weekend and tore up the application for a bank loan.

Our relief was short lived. We soon discovered that the rose-breasted grosbeaks had told the evening grosbeaks, and the purple finches had invited the gold; that the starlings had had a change of heart; and that, perversely and unaccountably, the sparrows had decided to switch from wild birdseed and table crumbs to sunflower seeds, forcing us to switch from sometime steak to frequent hot dogs.

We began to buy in still larger quantities. "Birds," our local naturalist wrote, "have to go to bed with full crops to survive the long winter nights."

"We don't smoke, drink, chew, go to movies, or gamble." Everett smiled weakly, easing a fifty-pound, fifteen-dollar bag of seed from the trunk of the car. Useless for me to remind him that even if we had the money or the inclination to live riotously, we no longer had the time nor the energy. It was all being spent on the birds.

There were times I wondered why. Especially on arctic January mornings when I stood at the window watching Everett, swathed in woolen robe, ear muffs and boots, as he plodded through three-foot drifts, a steaming kettle in each hand, on his way to melt the ice in the birds' watering trough. *Their* water before *his* coffee.

I questioned our sanity, too, in the spring, after the final thaw, when the two of us raked and shoveled and filled countless bags with sodden sunflower seed husks for pickup by Going Garbage — at a dollar a bag.

13

But my whys are only fleeting irritations, born of laziness and rheumatics. They evaporate as we watch our pair of devoted cardinals descend for dinner; or when our magnificent pileated woodpeckers, surfeited with suet, bugle their "So long! We're off!" Or when a pert chickadee perches on my outstretched hand and gives me a trusting onceover before helping itself to a tidbit.

Moments such as these bring to mind the charge of Father Zossima in *The Brothers Karamazov:* "Love all God's creation, the whole and every grain of sand in it. Love every leaf, every ray of light. Love the plants, the animals, love everything." An easy commandment, that.

Occasionally Everett, helping me slice oranges for the orioles, or watching me boil up a batch of hummingbird nectar, or roll peanut butter confections for the blue jays, will question the wisdom of our all-consuming interest, looking to me for justification of our extravagant hobby.

"Oh, come on! It's not been in vain," I reassured him one winter afternoon. "We've learned the pecking order of more than thirty species of birds, for one thing. We've learned to accept the beauty of their presence in lieu of gratitude —"

"And," he broke in, "we've learned that the best things in life are pretty expensive. Nothing at all like 'tuppence a bag.' " And with that he stomped off to find his pocket calculator, returning with the shocking proposition that if I would concoct an appetizing recipe for four and twenty blackbirds baked within a pastry shell, he would find a way to snare them!

We worked out a compromise that year by not buying a color TV. Last year we practiced the same economy for the same reason. Now it's decision time again and we toss the question back and forth. If we board up our feeders, the birds still have time to find other foraging spots before the snows arrive—and we can order our television, twice postponed.

We argue into the night. To feed or not to feed, that is the question. Or is it? Whom are we trying to kid? We know who will win. The dramatic black and yellow grosbeaks—sixty of them last year—that's who! And the raucous, vivid-blue jays. The checkered, immaculate hairies. And there's always the possibility that our pileated pair will return.

If we're lucky we can hold our fragile goldfinches through the winter and watch the alchemy that spring works on their plumage. And in the hush of winter, the black-capped, buff-breasted chickadees will wax bold and we will train them again to our hands—and who will care at a time like that that Koppel and Cousteau are in black and white? Not us! We'll settle again for the living color outside our kitchen windows!

2

Five Miles Per

IT IS NOT ALWAYS POSSIBLE TO "live in a house by the side of the road and be a friend of man." There are sometimes extenuating circumstances, such as blaring stereos, barking dogs, and speeding cars on dusty roads, that preclude the possibility. Especially speeding cars on dusty roads.

Sam Walter Foss wrote his poem a long time ago — in fact, before Henry Ford's Model T's began to roll off the assembly lines — and thus there was no way he could anticipate the problem. And, conditioned by a lifetime in the asphalt jungle of Chicago, neither could we. Our mobile home is situated on a strait of land betwixt two roads. They are not secondary or tertiary roads; they are improved cowpaths strewn with low-grade gravel and top-grade potholes. They are hub-deep in mud during the rainy season, snow-packed from December through March, and fallow in dust the rest of the year.

It is the "rest of the year" that brings out our hostility; that makes us — sorry, Sam Walter — "sit in the scorner's seat and hurl the cynic's ban." For most of our neighbors will never learn the simple scientific principle that the height of the dust cloud they raise as they drive down the lane is in direct proportion to the speed at which they travel.

Our mobile court clings to the edge of Highway 42 as it winds between Sister Bay and Ellison Bay. The coupes, the wagons, the vans, the pick-ups hurtle into our wooded court directly from the highway where the speed limit is 55, the drivers' feet still heavy on the pedals, their minds preoccupied with the business they have left behind in town or the tasks that await at home. Most of them are oblivious to the fact that before they have traveled 100 yards, they have passed several large caution signs reading 5 MPH, black on white, big as life. Nor do they notice the appeal to conscience that appears further along. *Slow,* it warns, *Children At Play.* But it has been here a long time, and the original kids at play have grown up without incident and are close to legal driving age themselves. The familiarity of the sign has bred contempt.

During my first summer in the dust bowl, I washed my fourteen windows every week. My husband tried to dissuade me, pointing out that by the time I got around to the fourteenth, number one already had a fine layer of silt coating its surface. I said I didn't care; that at least my conscience was clear, even if my windows weren't. Indoors, I dusted and vacuumed daily, but by nightfall I could write memos to myself on any polished surface in the house.

Our second summer I spent less time cleaning and more time praying for rain. Everett suggested that I pray for a more charitable spirit while I was at it because my hostility was showing.

"Remember," he admonished. "Inasmuch as is in you, you are to live peaceably with others."

I turned for support to my cross-the-road neighbor, Mrs. T. We'd meet outdoors, sometimes her yard, sometimes ours, once or twice a day to exchange complaints — she

18

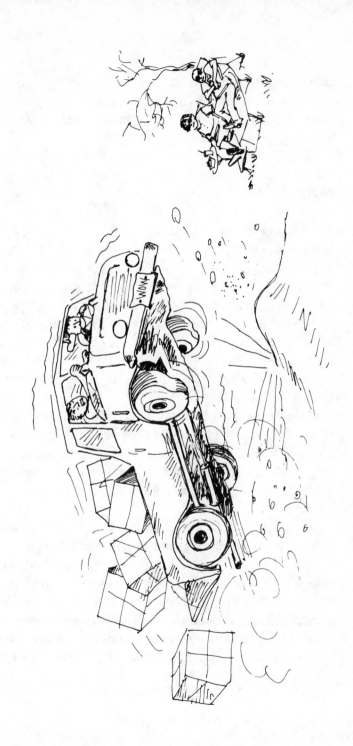

about having to wash dishes before as well as after meals, and I about the dust's disastrous effects on my sinus. We'd pause only long enough to glare at every driver who sped by breaking the dust barrier.

Mrs. T. was a woman of action. I'm sure it was a phone call from her to the powers-that-be that resulted in a letter's being sent to all the court residents reminding them to observe the speed regulations — a reminder that was every bit as effective as the posted signs.

I suspect it was Mrs. T. who subsequently suggested to our landlord that he get out his bulldozer and build a few speed bumps along the dusty lanes. Not being constructed of re-inforced concrete, they lasted only a few weeks, but they were an entertaining few weeks, I'll tell the world, as we sat in our yard sipping lemonade, watching unsuspecting visitors and absent-minded neighbors and UPS and GTE trucks hit the ramparts. It was a gratifying sight. Even Everett got a bang out of it!

Unfortunately, it was too much of a nuisance to maintain this system of ridges — or maybe a loud protest from our rural mail carrier (and our worst offender) carried weight — because they were never replaced once they were worn down, and we were soon back to eating and breathing dust.

Well, the speed bumps had been just the comic relief needed to return me to a more peaceable frame of mind. I decided that perhaps our crop-dusting neighbors would respond to a gentle and gracious reminder; perhaps a soft answer would turn away wrath and keep down the dust. I reasoned from a bend-over-backward stance that it is difficult to remember to slow to a crawl when one lives at the end of the road several hundred yards away. What I would do was try a little animated visual education.

So I posted myself at the edge of our lawn, holding a rake or a hoe or a weed cutter to justify my presence, and when a vehicle approached, I held up a hand with my fingers spread out, smiling all the while to demonstrate that I was a friendly persuader. Now to me, that gesture stood for "five," as in "miles per hour"; but I soon discovered that to the motorists it signified a neighborly "Hi, y'all!", and so they waved back as they sped on by — in a cloud of dust.

I reviewed my strategy and resolved to eliminate the smile. Instead I scowled as I held up my five fingers, scowled and shook my head disapprovingly. This brought to bay two speeders. They stopped and I aired my grievance at the top of my silt-clogged lungs and over their pulsating motors. They promised to mend their ways; even managed to sound a bit contrite; and they did slow down considerably from then on — every time they saw me in my yard.

The rest of the offenders continued to interpret my outstretched hand as a greeting, either out of ignorance or perversity, and because Everett said I was embarrassing him with my wooden Indian road show, I abandoned that attempt to consider others.

I wondered about a Burma Shave sign campaign, and I lay awake nights composing verses that might possibly slow down the traffic. Verses like "If Speed You Must, You'll Raise the Dust!" Or, "Let Sleeping Dust Lie, When You Drive By!" And for the younger generation: "Raise Flowers, Not Dust!" But the courage of my convictions weakened in the light of day. I abandoned that idea and returned to murmurings at home and therapeutic gripe sessions with Mrs. T.

Finally, in the middle of a long, hot, dry spell, Everett

21

cracked. Either from listening to a running recital of complaints from me or maybe just being tired of driving a car that looked as though it spent most of its hours in a gravel pit. At any rate, he took matters into his own hands. Ignoring the latest bulletin that warned residents not to water their grass or wash their cars because of the low water level, he uncoiled about sixty feet of garden hose and turned on the tap. He watered down the roads to the north and south of us. He turned up the pressure and sprinkled into mud all the dust that lay alongside of Mrs. T.'s domain. He did this three times a day for three days while I cowered behind the living room drapes waiting for a cease-and-desist order from our landlord.

On the morning of the fourth day, a county truck rumbled into the court; a man got out, opened up some spigots at the rear of the vehicle, climbed back in and drove on, spraying behind him a thick layer of oil. The dust was laid! It may have been coincidence. Everett is positive it was a clear case of cause and effect. I prefer to think it was the last straw for our beleagured laird. That was the end of the dust for the rest of the summer. Not that the air was clear — we were left with a strong, heavy odor of petroleum. And there was black "gum" on my linoleum and in my rugs — and on Poquito's pads.

Torrential rains came at the end of August and washed away the oil. After a windy and dry September the dust returned. I sat beneath my clematis vine on a fall evening when the sun was just hanging on the horizon. One of our chronic speeders raced by in his low-slung Pacer. The rays of the setting sun, filtered through the dust cloud he had raised, bathed everything in a golden glow.

Ah, well, I thought. *If you can't beat it, you might as well*

22

develop a philosophy about it. Like Aesop's fox and his unreachable grapes. So I sat and thought about Hamlet at the grave of Alas-poor-Yorick, sifting the ashes through his fingers and reflecting that the dust of Imperial Caesar, mixed with a little water, might somewhere be stopping up a hole "to keep the wind away."

I ran a finger over a leaf from my vine and looked at the dust I had gathered. Who knows? Maybe I was holding in my hand the quarks of dinosaurs and pterodactyls or a Potawatomi chieftain or a brother-in-law of Eric the Red!

Dust, when considered esthetically or scientifically or philosophically, does not seem anymore to be the scourge of a housewife's existence.

3

Our Blue Heaven

THERE IS A FRAGILE summer shack on highway 42 in the village of Gill's Rock that causes a traffic slow-down during the tourist season. It's not the cottage itself that catches the eye, for it is a nondescript and humble structure — an outsized playhouse, half-hidden by foliage and sill-deep in unmowed grass. What makes this wee cabin a minor tourist distraction is the audacious sign that the owners have fastened to its facade — a proclamation in bold, block letters that reads: Our Piece Of The Rock!

I applaud that kind of arrogance. How dull to live in a house by the side of the road with only a fire number for an identity. Seven years ago when Everett and I moved into our fourteen-by-seventy-foot mobile home, I could hardly wait to hold a christening ceremony. I wanted to smash a beribboned Coke bottle across the hitch and shout something like "I dub thee *Reichels' Roost!* Or *Our Escape Hutch!* Or *Pied-A-Terre!*" However, we never got around to a ritualized launching of our shoebox because we couldn't agree on a name that was clever without being cute, solid without being pretentious.

As a result of our procrastination, we ended up with a funereal claim marker, a flat rock about the size and shape of a modest headstone, our name splashed rudely across its surface in green paint. Each spring we dig it out of the mud and prop it up next to the driveway. Between the rapacious snow-on-the-mountain that grows affectionately around and over it, and the pot of geraniums on its left flank, the site has the appearance of a well-tended grave. Our lack of inventiveness was a constant source of embarrassment to me until one day a visitor — an English teacher at that — gazed long and hard at our headstone and finally marveled: "Clever! Very clever! A symbolic suggestion that your retirement home is your final resting place!"

Whereas Everett is crazy about the Forest Lawn image, I am all for throwing the rock back into the lake and resuming our quest for a name. "It's not too late," I remind him as we scour the countryside on Sunday afternoons via bike, moped, or car. Now that Door County has become a realtor's paradise, with new homes replacing apple and cherry orchards as the main scenic attractions, personalizing one's domicile with a name carved in wood or scrolled in rosemaling has become *the* thing to do. And hunting clever toponyms has replaced collecting epitaphs as a quiet Sabbath diversion. For us, that is.

When we first began pedaling down the back roads nine years ago, we were intrigued by a sign that the sun and rain have since almost obliterated. Now, it takes a second, closer inspection to make sure it still says *Coffee's Grounds*. There are some names that suggest and even demand a certain combination, and the Coffees surrendered to the inevitable. So did the Martens, summertime residents on county B, a migrating flock, who inform the passing motorists that their place is *The Martens' Nest*.

We found that a lot of home owners prefer alliteration to

26

punning, like the Martens' neighbors who have dubbed their place *Holler's Hollow*; and the folks along Beach Road who share *Donald's Duck-A-Way.*

Then there's the resident, a year-round native with a broad sense of humor, who capitalizes on his name — at the same time making a bid for fame — by the handsome sign he has erected on his property at the junction of ZZ and Old Stage. It is a sign that looks as though it might have been planted there by the state historical society declaring that therein lives:

GRIEF ERICKSON
THE FOUNDER OF APPLEPORT

The sign's credibility is enhanced by the log homestead Erickson completed a few years ago, but which appears to be a well-preserved pioneer settlement, circa 1850. Don "Grief" Erickson is entitled to do a little leg-pulling; he has left a legacy in his labor of love.

Occasionally we drive down the short and lonely North Bay Road. "Lonely," Everett maintains, "because the mosquitoes tend to discourage human visitation." But from behind the closed windows of the station wagon it is a pleasant drive past swamps and cathedral woods, ending at a tranquil bay. Just before the macadam gives way to gravel there is a meadow in the middle of which a Norseman announced his proprietorship by erecting a wooden plaque that read *Landsman's Fält.* I was reasonably certain that "Fält" translated to "field," but to save embarrassment I had my husband check it out with a Swedish friend. Now, *Landsman's Fält* by itself is not remarkable; however, a few acres away, a wit capitalized on it by tagging his estate *Nobody's Fault!*

There's another cynic who calls his property on the

Valmi turn on the way to Sturgeon Bay, *Belly Acres!*, causing us to wonder if the house is inhabited by chronic complainers or whether it was one horrendous back-breaking project just getting the place together.

Wordplay is popular on signposts. The Lowells — was it an act of desperation? — called their place *The Last Resort.* And then there's the family who spends its summers at *Holidaze.* They, in turn, have upbeat neighbors who like to think of their spread as *Happy Ours.*

When we see the *Clarks At Last!* signpost, we speculate. Was it christened *after* the mortgage burning? Or is it merely an expression of rapture that evolved over years of long commutes from the city, of crawling out of crowded, vacation-packed cars, stretching away the kinks and inhaling the balsam-scented air and the lake breezes, impulsively exclaiming, ''Clark's, at last!''

We can empathize with the Clarks as well as with the Nelsons, whose summer place is their *Home Port*; and with the family who waxed poetic with *Little Heaven By The Sea;* and with the escapists who call their shore cottage *Mmmmmm, So Nice!* Oh, well we know! How many Friday nights have we pulled in alongside our mobile home in the woods, bone-weary from the six-hour drive on top of a full workday, and found ourselves instantly revived by the first deep breath of fresh air this side of Chicago and the spectacle of a star-studded sky overhead and the clear call of a whippoorwill as we placed our key in the lock! Mmmmm, so nice!

Some house signs proclaim the obvious, like the redundant *The Larsons Live Here.* Or the cottage with eighteen windows, every one of which is framed in bright blue shutters, and whose appellation is — what else, but —*The Blue Shutters?*

29

I love the airy-fairiness of *Sand Castles* in the Sevastopol Dunes on the Lake Michigan side of the peninsula, a locale rich in place names. For sure it must be a young and clever lawyer who calls his home *The Legal Pad!* It surprises me that the M.D. around the bend hasn't followed suit with *The Prescription Pad* — a quadruple entendre! Instead, he has chosen the ingenious *Off Call,* which makes me wonder if his telephone is unlisted and if he leaves his beeper back in the city.

There are Old World names, like *Stonecroft.* Is the owner British? Literary? Sardonic? Or a little of each? To tell the truth, there isn't an acre of land in our particular section of the peninsula that couldn't bear the name *Stonecroft*; a field of stone, a stony farm. There are three *"Stonecrofts"* within a pebble's toss of each other; four, if I count *Ty Cerrig* in the town of Sister Bay. *Ty Cerrig,* Welsh for "a stone house" or "a house built on rocks."

Tan Y Bwlch (try "tahn ee bookh") is another Welsh phrase, this one posted at the entrance to the Williams's oasis on the bay south of Bailey's Harbor. It is a nostalgic name, borrowed from a grandfather's farm in Wales and brought here to keep the memory alive of a farm "at the foot of a hill."

Another tantalizing cognomen is that on the Ballantyne's summer place on North Bay, an idyllic cove. *Auld Lum Reekie* it reads. Now, *"Auld Reekie"* I recognized as an affectionate, descriptive nickname for the old city of Edinburgh with its smoky chimneys and acrid stench. I took a second look at the shallow bay on which the cottage is situated and wondered if there could be a sulfuric miasma that arises from its surface of a morning. But it seems there is a Gaelic benediction, "May your lums always reek!"

Translated: "May your chimneys always smoke!" Paraphrased: "May you never run out of fuel!" An apt blessing in this day of short supplies and soaring prices!

Some folks just west of us labeled their place *Afterthought*. I shall have to knock on their door some day and ask what they meant. Most of *my* afterthoughts arrive too late to be of any use. Perhaps as an afterthought they ought to add a clarifying word or two to clear up the mystery.

Someone did that on a back road in Ephraim — tacked on a postscript, I mean. They named their retreat *Hidden Acres*. The passage of time must have proved that to be only too true, for later they added three words that will ensure their company finds them. The amended sign now reads: *Hidden Acres (End of Lane)*.

It is poignantly appropriate that on the outskirts of this same village there should be a place called *"Stillmeadows,"* for it was here in Ephraim that the writer Glady's Taber, of Stillmeadow fame, spent her summers with her family. I'm glad someone remembered.

Almost across the road from *Stillmeadows,* down a steep, wooded lane is a homestead that bears the name *Herlig Utsigt*. I met a troll there who told me it meant "beautiful view," and I couldn't argue with him, for it overlooks the sunset bay at Ephraim and the wooded bluff of Peninsula Park.

When we have only a half hour for a bike ride, we like to take what we call the Roen Orchard trail. It's a circle tour that keeps us off the highway and on a wind-swept ridge bordered by apple orchards, over to Beach Road, a shadowy lane that twists and turns through deep woods. Near the end of the trail there's a new home, a log cabin that appears to have grown there naturally along with the hundreds of evergreens that someone had the foresight to plant before laying the house's foundation.

There is an honest and tranquil aura that surrounds the cabin. I am in love with its roofed porch and shining windows, and every time I pedal past, I break a commandment — I covet my neighbor's house! In a year or two, the young pines will hide the cabin completely from view, but the signpost on the shoulder of the road will be there to remind us that the Coxes live there, Doug and Sonja, and what's more, their house is *Shared With God!*

"That's my favorite sign," I confide to my husband as we ride side by side on a fall afternoon.

He snorts. It is his opinion that I am highly capricious as well as greedy. "*Your* favorite sign," he contradicts me, "is the one that says *For Sale!*"

I ignore his taunt and fall into a reverie, remembering a story from out of Everett's prehistoric past when he was the teacher of a women's Bible class in the Poconos. The study group met once a week in the homes of the various members. One of the dear ladies, Alice Waterman, invariably welcomed her guests with "Now, don't you mind how things look; we're only camping here!"

That always triggered a laugh, because Mrs. Waterman's housekeeping was beyond reproach, and there was nothing to apologize for. Those who knew her love for the Lord realized that the expression "we're only camping" was more than just a quip — she was referring to her conviction that her citizenship was not in that quiet, elm-lined street in Stroudsburg, Pennsylvania, but in the courts of heaven.

We share that feeling of transience — it's a part of the

Christian experience. Perhaps that's why we haven't come up with a clever name for our retirement home — our roots are shallow and our lease is short. That 25-pound stone on which I daubed our name years ago has been adequate; the UPS trucks, the mailman, and the occasional visitor from our former life all find us by that faded inscription. But if we ever do replace it, we have a phrase handy, provocative, and profound. We'll have it burned in wood, and it will swing from the oak tree that shades the small rock garden. *The Reichels' Way Station,* it will read, and when the curious stop to ask its significance, we will tell them that a couple of wayfarers are stopping here on their way to heaven.

4

The P.O.R. Race

I WAS IN MY EIGHTH WEEK of a stubborn, hacking cough
and down to the dregs of my third bottle of Formula 44D.
Everything I ate tasted of Sucrets, and I wore a long-
outgrown girdle to prevent a hernia or a cracked rib. Having
been cured once before of a lingering and debilitating bronchitis by a sojourn in Michigan's Upper Peninsula, I
suggested, and Everett agreed, that we should try the
"cure" again. My husband cautioned that it would have to
be a short trip, however; we couldn't afford the expense or
the time for more than a long weekend. We'd leave on
Thursday and return home on Saturday or Sunday.

We hadn't been back to the Copper Country since the last
time our four children, all grown now, had been with us in
our rented cottage on Lake Michigamme. As we drove
north, we recognized familiar landscapes, and the memories
of our family's encounters with deer, snakes, bear, and lake
storms came flooding back.

By late afternoon we were settled into a motel. We went
to bed early with early rising in mind. If the beautiful
weather held, we would eat lunch the next day on the shores
of awesomely lovely Lake Fanny Hooe. The weather coop-

erated; and the cheese and rolls, the Twinkies and orange juice we picked up at the Copper Harbor grocery were a gourmet feast in the crisp autumn air — air that was redolent of balsam and pine, cedar and tamarack. "Healthful" air, the World Book encyclopedia calls it. We lay there in the sun-dappled grass listening to the rustle of dry leaves and the plopping of the leaping fish.

The tall bluff across the lake, on its west shore, shortens the day at the park. Reluctantly we tore ourselves away, driving back along the west shore of the peninsula, sparkling Lake Superior on our right. A doe watched us from the shadows around a turn; further along we braked at the rare sight of a timber wolf loping across the road; we discovered the ghost town of Mandan — a place we had searched for many times before with no success — and walked its deserted streets.

"One more stop," I begged. I wanted to make a pilgrimage to the lakeside cottage where the children and I had spent a summer some twenty years before. After several wrong turns, we found the gravel road out of Champion. A few miles, a sharp turn-off, and there it was! Deserted, in disrepair, the house was boarded up against vandals. The barn in which the children had played on rainy days was totally flattened. We didn't linger; it was no longer the happy place I had remembered.

Everett started the car and shifted into reverse, deciding to back down the short lane to the gravel road. When he thought he had gone far enough, he began to turn. There was a sickening, scraping sound, and we came to a jolting stop. We were hung up on a boulder. A pair of husky Good Samaritans came by and insisted on lending a hand. By the time they were finished with us, we were totally incapaci-

The P.O.R. Races

tated, and they left me behind while they drove my husband to town to call for a tow truck.

The woods were somber and hostile in the ebbing light — and so was I. What had begun as an idyllic weekend had ended in a fiasco! I sat in the disabled car feeling very sorry for myself. I was angry with Everett for backing instead of turning. I was angry with God for letting it happen. I was also angry with myself for not being able to accept this vicissitude with grace.

The mechanic towed us twenty-five miles to his garage where our crippled car was put in drydock until parts could be ordered from Green Bay and the repairs made. Since this was a Friday evening and nothing would be open until Monday, our mangled drive shaft would not be repaired and replaced until Wednesday or Thursday. We were dropped off at a motel across the road from the garage, and the mechanic pointed out the shopping plaza a quarter of a mile away. "It has a lunch counter," he said, "and they serve a ninety-nine-cent breakfast." Everett perked up noticeably at that information. Breakfast is his favorite time of day.

That evening, my spirits were at their lowest ebb. Resentment, reproach, and self-pity taking turns at eroding my morale, I lay in bed and watched the ten o'clock news. The sports segment featured something called a P.O.R. Race that was to be run the next day in the Keweenaw area — a race over unimproved back roads, logging trails, and abandoned jeep ruts into the interior. Teams of two men, a driver and a navigator, rode in standard passenger cars. During the course of the race (which followed paved roads only when absolutely necessary) the cars had to cross boulder-strewn creeks, climb over or around rocks and fallen trees, churn through swamps and spin their way out of sand traps. The

P.O.R., the sportscaster explained, stood for "Press on regardless!"

"They're crazy!" I informed my spouse who was doubled over in laughter at some of the footage being shown from a previous race. "They're a bunch of masochists!" At that point I could not see anything heroic or humorous about the purposeful wrecking of a perfectly good car.

"Oh, I don't know. Looks like a lot of fun to me. After all, that's what it's all about, isn't it? The obstacles, I mean? Overcoming them! Reaching the finishing line! Proving the toughness of man and machine! Pressing on regardless!"

I popped another Sucret into my mouth and pulled the covers up around my chin. " 'Press on Regardless!' Sounds to me like something from Kipling or Alfred, Lord Tennyson," I grumbled. " 'Half a league, half a league, Half a league onward, All in the valley of death, Rode the six hundred.' Pressing on regardless!"

"Sounds more to me like something from the Bible."

"It *does* have an authoritative ring," I admitted. "Like something Paul might have said."

"Like something Paul *did* say. Like 'I press toward the mark for the prize of the high calling of God in Christ Jesus!' " Everett quoted, somewhat complacently.

I, too, recalled a press-on-regardless quotation originating with Paul, but my cough medicine and the events of the day were having a soporific effect on my memory, and since I could produce only a reasonable facsimile, I kept it to myself: "I don't consider anything that happens to me in this life of any consequence; I just want to finish my race with joy!" That paraphrase cut a little too close for comfort, so I switched off the bedside lamp, pulled the covers over

39

my head, and fell asleep, postponing my confrontation with conviction until a more convenient time.

We ate our breakfasts that week at the supermarket counter and afterwards hiked along the country roads. We went to Ishpeming for lunches and window shopping, accommodatingly transported by the Senior Citizens' bus. We dined out of cans and jars in our motel room, much to the delight of Poquito, a hobo at heart. Everett spent his afternoons hovering around the garage and talking to a relative of the mechanic, an elderly man whose faith was in need of shoring up. I spent my time alone thinking and reading, and a good portion of my cogitating was concentrated on those initials, that intriguing P.O.R., along with Everett's challenge: "That's what it's all about, isn't it? The obstacles?"

I am just as deceitful and desperately wicked as the next person, and the one I delude most often is myself. So at first I held it at arm's length, that clever P.O.R., saying to myself, "What a brilliant idea for a sermon! I must share it with our pastor." Next, the pragmatic in me surfaced, and I decided, "That's a fascinating idea, that P.O.R. Race, for a magazine article! *Guideposts* ought to like it."

But, finally, about the fourth day of our enforced retreat, I reached the point where I felt that the race had been run and bally-hooed on TV expressly for me. Me, sulking in my motel room over a minor accident in which neither of us had been hurt, and for which Colonial Penn would pay in due time! The truth is, I tend to fall apart at obstacles; more so now that I am approaching what the Preacher labeled "the evil days." This is not a boast; it is a confession.

Everett had reminded me that the P.O.R. racers gloried in obstacles. Not me! I would have gone home after the first blowout. Never mind that obstacles was the name of the game. "Life is difficult enough in my own back yard," I would say from my heart. "I don't need these added aggravations!"

And if Everett wasn't quick enough to retort, my own conscience would probably have reminded me that Paul also rejoiced in obstacles, "knowing that tribulation [or overcoming obstacles, if you will] brings about perseverance; and perseverance, proven character; and proven character, hope; and hope does not disappoint, because the love of God has been poured out within our hearts through the Holy Spirit who was given to us."*

We drove home with our drive shaft as good as new and my bronchia likewise; but the sanctified indomitability, the power to persevere so that I can finish my course with joy, were still a long way out of reach. I was not being entirely facetious when I told Everett that I was going to paste the letters P.O.R. on the wall behind my Underwood where I open my mail and read my rejection slips; another set on the base of the telephone where I talk to the children scattered all over the continent and listen to their problems long-distance; a third monogramed on the dashboard of our four-year-old station wagon, laboring under the weight of its 123,000 miles and letting me know about it by strange noises and ominous odors. And it wouldn't hurt to decorate the bathroom mirror with the P.O.R. emblem. Not in my house, it wouldn't.

Alas, I am a slow learner, petty and impatient. I have yet to master the lesson that it is in the obstacles of life that I can prove the sufficiency of God. If I had no conflicts, no setbacks, no dark valleys, no broken drive shafts, there would be no call for me to press on regardless. I would not

*Romans 5:3-5, *New American Standard Bible* (NASB)

require the services of a Shepherd, a Counselor, a Comfort-
er, a Burden-bearer, nor would I have need for a God who
said, "I am the Lord. Is there anything too hard for Me?"

Nor would I ever be able to say with any credibility: "I
can do all things through Christ which strengtheneth me."

5

Poquito, Our Logo

WE TAKE GOOD CARE OF OUR DOG, stopping just this side of pampering. Our solicitous concern for our pooch surprises a lot of people in this farming community in northeastern Wisconsin, where Labradors and Newfoundlands are the norm. It surprises them because Poquito, our ten-year-old-Chihuahua, appears to have no redeeming qualities whatsoever—other than a slavish devotion to my husband and me. She can't round up cattle, flush pheasant, or keep the squirrels out of the bird feeders. And in addition to being good for naught, she is anti-social in the extreme.

Before her first birthday had rolled around, she had selected her own society—our immediate family—and then shut the door. All other human beings since then are suspect and fair game. Animals, likewise, with one exception. At the age of six months, she fell in love with a sniveling white French poodle, Pierre. It was only a brief encounter on an Ozark vacation, but she has been a pushover for white poodles ever since. No other breed need apply.

One of our reasons for maintaining Poquito in the pink of condition is that she is a lapdog (when we sit) and a hiphugger (when we recline), and that kind of proximity demands that we keep her free of fleas, ticks, and sarcoptic mange. It also explains why I shampoo her fairly often. When she ceases to smell like warm, buttered toast, and both her pelt and my husband's clothes take on a doggy odor, I turn on the taps and summon her to her bath.

Not only do we try to keep her squeaking clean, we both work hard at seeing that she is comfortably warm. Poquito is a long-coated Chihuahua who functions best at an indoor temperature of 75 degrees. Because our thermostat is set at 70, she spends most of the winter in a turtle-necked sweater, in partial hibernation under an afghan on the living room sofa.

We confess that we dote on our dog — and that would be reason enough to keep her warm and clean and well-fed. "*Too* well-fed," accuses the vet. Like us, she is getting older and more sedentary, and that, coupled with a decreasing metabolic efficiency, necessitates her being on a special diet with vitamin supplements and a lecithin additive to help dissolve the fatty deposits that she harbors subcutaneously. Oh, that *our* adipose tissues were so easily melted!

"She's got another eight or nine years in her," prognosticates the doc as he fills an envelope with pills.

Happily we tuck her under an arm and head for home. Those eight or nine years are important to us, not merely because we love her, but because she has become our logo. We live in a community teeming with bespectacled, white-thatched senior citizens. To a newcomer we all look alike. Whatever variations there are in height or width are not dramatic enough to facilitate differentiation. And when every third person is a Nelson or a Carlson or an Anderson, the problem is compounded.

To be wall-eyed or a stutterer or to have six fingers on each hand would be an advantage in the identity crisis. To have a golden-coated Chihuahua with her own special car seat next to the driver, and who accompanies us almost everywhere, has helped separate us from the common herd. We have become known as "that old couple in the green station wagon with the little dog in the front seat." In the summer months we are likely to be pointed out as "that old couple on bikes who take their little dog along in a basket."

Poquito makes such a dramatic impression leaning into the wind from her handlebar perch, so obviously enjoying the excursion, scouring the countryside for animal life to challenge, that when we do leave her home, we are stopped by indignant folk who want to know why.

Rusty, the stock boy and bagger at the Beach Road Market, never fails to carry our groceries to the car in order to spend a few minutes in conversation with Poquito. Not that she encourages him. When anyone other than next of kin approaches the family chariot she assumes the ferocity of a Doberman, baring her fangs and rocking the car with her noisy hostility. This delights Rusty, who recognizes the act for what it is, pure bravado, and so reaches in boldly to scratch her ears while she continues to snarl and protest the trespass. Thanks to Poquito, Rusty recognizes us among all the other senior citizens at church, and it is a pleasure to have a teenager go out of his way to greet us in a crowd, even if it is merely to ask, "How's Poquito?"

The ranger at the Newport Park wilderness area sees a lot of station wagons in the course of a year, but ours is the only one that harbors an automatic, animated burglar alarm. Even if we weren't so conspicuously the first skiers of the season — and quite often the last — Ranger Stahl would still remember us, not for our cross-country enthusiasm, but for our "pesty dog that won't stop barking long enough for a

45

person to get a word in edgewise." And Everett can testify that there are a couple of state police on the County S speedtrap who would agree that we have not taught our Mexican spitfire proper respect for authority.

Poquito has become a necessary adjunct locally; a symbol, an ice breaker, a conversation piece. However, our primary reason for doing all we can to ensure her longevity is not merely to maintain an identity around the northern tip of our particular peninsula, but rather to guarantee us a solid place in the memories of our Canadian grandchildren.

With two sets of long-distance grandparents, paternal in California and my husband and me in Wisconsin, our young Quebeckian grandchildren sometimes have difficulty keeping us separated in their thinking. It was inevitable that we would become "the Grandma and Grandpa who live with Poquito." That way everything falls into place for them: our house, with Poquito asleep on the sofa; our yard, with Poquito pursuing a chipmunk; and us, with Poquito in the lap of one or the other.

As for the California grandparents, they are going to have to adopt an ostrich, stable a pony, or add some bizarre dimension to their lives if they don't want to be recalled as the lackluster "Grandma and Grandpa who *don't* live with Poquito!"

6

We'll Take the Road Less Traveled!

WE HAD BEEN A LITTLE RELUCTANT to go biking, afraid of the traffic on the Fourth of July weekend. Winter and spring had spoiled us to the point that we considered the roads congested if we met three or four cars on our ten-mile round trip down Old Stage Road. Today we didn't want to have to inhale exhaust fumes from passing vehicles as we labored uphill and coasted down; nor did we want to have to observe the rules of the road at every intersection.

We are accustomed to sailing right past stop signs — after a good look in each direction as we approach — an infraction I justify by admitting that most of my falls have occurred while I was stopping or starting out. I am like an airplane, Everett tells me, in that I am in greater peril on take offs and landings than while I am in motion.

On this particular weekend we were gratified to find that once we walked our bikes across the busy highway, we had our old country roads to ourselves. What's more, the air was sweet — a potpourri from the young orchards at Swanson's farm, the dark woods on Green Road, and the knee-high corn at Kalm's Hill. The sun was hot on our shoulders, and only occasionally, when a stronger current of air moved across the road from the west where the highway paralleled our route, did we hear the heavy traffic of the vacationers; but it was only a hum, and a transitory one at that.

"We should have remembered," I called out to Everett. "The tourists don't take the back roads!"

He smiled and waved in agreement as he pulled ahead. We were going to have a beautiful "bike" after all.

Bicycling on the back roads is the ideal way to tour our hilly peninsula. Biking has an obvious advantage over walking; at least a ten-to-one advantage if one rides racing bikes as we do. In some respects it beats motoring because it is the perfect pace, our seven to eight miles per hour, for philosophizing, meditating, and for working one's way out of a writing block. The landscape passes by slowly enough to be taken in and enjoyed, and the distractions are only pleasant ones—except for an occasional farm dog out to relieve his boredom by intimidating anything on wheels.

Whenever I find myself in a blue funk or tensions begin to build, I mount my Motobecane—specially geared by Steve, the bicycle and ski man, to get me up all but the steepest hills—and I pedal down the road past Swanson's, on and up to the crest of the peninsula where I pause to feed my soul on the vista of woods and meadows and sparkling inlets. Then a long coast, almost a mile, down to Mink River Road, a left turn next and a winding, easy pedal into the village of Ellison Bay.

There I pick up a can of cold pop to slake my thirst before starting back home. It is better than a whole bottle of Valium, that seven-mile tour. Better than Aldomet or Esimil for bringing down the blood pressure. I suspect Robert Louis Stevenson traveled by shank's mare rather than by bicycle, but I share his sentiment: "All I ask, the heaven above, And the road below me."

48

Every summer, inspired by tales of epic
achievement in *Modern Maturity,* I suggest to
Everett that we tour the entire peninsula — by bike.

Five years ago, and every summer since then, inspired no doubt by tales of epic achievement in *Modern Maturity,* I suggested to Everett that we cover the entire peninsula — every navigable mile of it — by bike. It is a delusion of grandeur and endurance that my husband wisely discourages, pointing out that the overall distance that we can pedal without strain seems to shrink a bit each year. Where we once dared twenty to twenty-five miles in an afternoon, we now consider ten an accomplishment. Our problem is not so much aging muscles as atrophy of will power.

Although we have not exactly put our racing bikes out to pasture, we find ourselves using them almost exclusively for exercise, relying on our Mopeds for pleasure, and relaxing in our five-year old Chevy for longer trips and inclement weather. However, whatever mode of transportation, we tend to travel the back roads. Even on our trips to the grocery store — whether north to Ellison Bay's Pioneer Market at 10 P.M. for the fixings for a late snack or into Sister Bay for a *Chicago Tribune* and a dozen eggs — we avoid highway 42 with its 55-mph limit and its no-nonsense, shortest-distance-between-two-points approach. We prefer the meandering, deep-shadowed Beach Road/Porcupine Bay Drive that follows the contours of the Green Bay shore.

Poquito, too, prefers the slower pace and the wooded terrain. She knows there are more dogs and deer to the linear mile along these quiet back stretches, and she strains like a foxhound ready for the chase, treading excitedly in place in her front seat platform. Who knows? Last night it was a mother skunk and her six kittens undulating across the road that made us stop with a squeal of brakes, just in time to avoid mass slaughter and suddenly enough to send Poquito somersaulting to the floor in the middle of a bark.

50

Next time it could be a porcupine or a raccoon, a deer or a gopher, and our aging pet has as much of a yen for adventure as her silver-haired owners.

"Where will it be today?" Everett asks, jingling the car keys. We plot our course more carefully now that gas prices have soared. We are more selective on our jaunts, not so apt any more to follow an unfamiliar lane merely out of curiosity. Rather, we retrace the old favorites — the tried and trues, the less traveled roads.

We have rationed ourselves two tankfuls a month. When Everett takes the dog out at night he checks the odometer and records the day's mileage on a chart on our kitchen bulletin board. We have come to think of ourselves as living a gallon of gas from the grocery store and the post office, two gallons from church, and eight gallons from the nearest metropolis, Sturgeon Bay.

Twice a month, duty calls us into Sturgeon Bay, and when we have enough gas — when the needle trembles slightly above the *E*, and not below it — we take roads G and B out of Egg Harbor. This meandering route follows the shores of Green Bay on the west side of the peninsula and begins by descending into the lush splendor of the Alpine Resort and golf course and ends at the duck pond on the outskirts of Sturgeon Bay.

In the miles between, there is a fascinating panorama of bluff and meadow; sparkling waters; majestic Old World barns; Murphy's Park, where we alight for a picnic lunch or just to stretch our legs and skip stones; mile upon mile of winding, wooded roads where homes are discreetly hidden behind cedar and pine; and then, hugging the bay shore, the "magnificent mile" or two of unique residences from gracious French Provincial to stark New England.

51

There are modern dwellings carved out of the bluffs by affluent "swallows;" and artist Gerhard Miller's oasis of loveliness that lures one into stopping — if the hours and the season are right — to partake of the treasures within as well. It's a beautiful way to travel to town on a prosaic shopping trip for yard goods or hardware or a visit to the dentist!

We fill up with gas and groceries after our business is taken care of, have a sandwich at McDonald's, and head for home. There's nothing wrong with taking highway 42 back north — except that almost everyone does. We prefer 57 that runs along the east shore until it cuts cross country at Bailey's Harbor. We're especially fond of the dappled, curving stretch north of Jacksonport; and if perchance traffic on 57 gets too heavy, we have an escape route, a tangent into another world.

Just before we reach Kangaroo Lake, south of Bailey's Harbor, I hold my breath to see if Everett is on the same wavelength. If he is, we make a sharp left onto Logerquist Road. There, for a few miles I can pretend we are motoring on Cape Breton or through England's Lake Country or in the center of one of Constable's landscapes. The owners of this acreage have thus far been able to keep it undisturbed and unspoiled. That they do so intentionally and with the highest of motives is borne out by the hand-wrought sign in one of the meadows: *How Nature Must Despair at Mankind Tearing at Her Hair!*

Well, along Logerquist Drive, Nature doesn't even get her tresses teased — yet.

Door County is shaped like a thumb, an elongated one that extends out into Lake Michigan. A forty-minute ferry boat ride from the tip of that thumb is Washington Island, originally an Icelandic settlement; now a tourist mecca. One of the two jumping-off places at the north end of the peninsula is Gill's Rock. Truckers and tourists, in a hurry to catch the next ferry, are preoccupied with passing the gawkers who have nothing more important on their minds than sight-seeing. It is a pass-or-be-passed two-lane stretch that we avoid during the summer season.

We bear left on the outskirts of Ellison Bay and take the Garrett Bay Road past the new post office and fire station and the old schoolhouse; past the Clearing, a woodland, year-round retreat; and past the *suburbia incipiens* growing around its fringes. We reach the Hardings's farm, where we have to make a decision because either way is lovely and will take us eventually to the same destination. The one on the left wanders a bit and is unpaved for the most part, but both of them promise to plunge us into a green undersea world in the summer, and a heart-stopping, words-fail-us canvas in the fall.

When the two roads merge again, still in the tunneled woods, we can see the lake scintillating on the horizon, and we watch for the short break in the trees and the ramp down to the water where scuba divers in bright orange, outlandish getup are setting out for a practice run. I shudder at their daring as I see them disappear beneath the waves, and I keep an eye on Everett, for he would join the submarine party at the drop of a flipper. Muddy, littered lake bottoms have always attracted him. He is convinced it is his destiny to cavort with mermaids and porpoises.

Washington Island is plainly visible on the horizon from the divers' ramp, and on our right we can watch the ferry boats chugging into Gill's Rock — a mere hailing distance across the water, but four or five miles along our back road. Last fall when the open lake was acting up, we came upon

53

an ore boat anchored in this sheltered bay, waiting for the storm to abate. Its hugeness dwarfed the harbor.

The ferry dock at Gill's Rock is a congested place in the summer; long lines of cars queue up on the left of the steep hill waiting their turn to board the *Eyrabakki* or the *Hans Richter*; others head back up the incline after disembarking, filled with wind-blown day visitors and cottagers whose vacation time has expired.

We don't intrude upon the busy settlement. Instead we turn right just at its brink to follow 42 to its northern terminus — Northport. Changing character as soon as it leaves the Rock, 42 is no longer an expeditious, traffic-clogged thoroughfare. It almost seems to say, "OK, I've done what I was supposed to do. Now let me have my head for the last mile or two."

And so from Gill's Rock to Northport, Highway 42 is a unique back road. A few years ago some engineers with a penchant for setting the crooked straight began surveying the last leg of this road, but public hue and cry — or was it lack of funding — saved the serpentine trail along whose length the power lines have stubbornly taken the shortest route, creating a most interesting effect.

Northport is aptly named; it is the winter port of call for the Washington Island ferry, during the time that Gill's Rock harbor is choked with ice. But in milder weather it has other attractions.

The long pier, extending several hundred feet into the lake, provides an excellent spot for a free car wash, providing there's a stiff breeze out of either the north or south. Since the nearest commercial car laundry is forty miles away, and car washing is discouraged in our mobile home court, we "go ecological" at Northport at every opportu-

54

nity. Everett sits in the wind-buffeted car, running the wipers after each new wave breaks over the roof, probably imagining himself in the pilot house of a fishing boat in the North Sea during a hurricane. Poquito and I walk along the beach, and I fill my pockets with pebbles, agates, and fossils.

The Northport pier is an ideal place from which to fish. The breeze at the end of the ramp keeps bugs to a minimum; the views of Plum and Pilot Islands, the ferry boats on the horizon, and the ore boats passing close enough so that the pulsing of their engines can be heard, all satisfy the romantic. True, I have yet to see anyone haul in anything large enough to fillet or mount, but the anglers all appear contented and comfy in their folding lawn chairs and straw hats, binoculars and bait at the ready.

If Everett ever lets me get a fishing license, that is where I will hang out for six months of the year. If he will come along with me, that is. So far, his reply to an invitation to dangle a worm is the same redundant one that he gives when invited to go golfing. "No thanks. I've already been there once before."

When we first came to Door County, there was a certain big-city naiveté that we had to shed. For one thing, we looked upon *Dead End* signs as official and as binding as *No Trespassing* warnings. Then one day, letting our curiosity do the navigating, we drove right past one, and we discovered Cana Island and a rich trove of thimbleberries. It is still labelled *Dead End*, but adventure lies at its "dead end," including a causeway that has to be waded in rough weather and a photogenic lighthouse.

Here it was we met our first orchard orioles; they escorted us around the island while we literally waded its circumfer-

55

ence on the shelf of rock that surrounds it. Along this stretch of road we often see deer and grouse, rabbits and hawks.

Emboldened, we followed other *Dead Ends* after that and discovered that they led to boat ramps on quiet bays or to sandy beaches. Some, to our embarrassment, have ended in private backyards — as did the Europe Lake trail where the *Dead End* was a private estate and we were challenged in a surly manner by a pair of custodians who weren't quite sure how best to intimidate a pair of grandparents already quaking in their boots.

Our only excuse, which we were not given time to offer, was that we *were* on skis, not wheels, and in cross-country gear one does get the Indian feeling that the earth belongs to all of us; or on an even more exalted plane, that "the earth is the Lord's and the fullness thereof" and nobody has the right to forbid a peaceful wayfarer passage.

Well, we beat a hasty retreat from that *Dead End,* so hasty that I took a clumsy tumble at the feet of our harassers, a gauche pancake when I wanted so badly to leave the scene gracefully and with dignity. When we arrived home, I comforted myself with a pot of hot chocolate while I read aloud to Everett from Robert Frost's "Mending Wall," that subtle jibe at those insecure folk who feel the need to build walls. But there is a happy footnote to this episode: a year ago this wildly beautiful and posted area became the property of Newport Wilderness Park, and now we can "trespass" to our heart's content!

Even a heavily frequented place like Peninsula State Park has its back roads. When the tourist population has thinned down in the fall, we return to the park. There is hardly an acre we haven't hiked, or skiied, or biked over — in our prime. Now we drive—to places like the Blossomburg Cemetery on Mengelberg Road, where I get out to read the old headstones and reflect on "flowers that waste their sweetness on the desert air." Everett dozes behind the wheel; he is not into epitaphs.

We are apt to drive from the cemetery to an isolated area in the center of the park where, until recently, there was a tumble-down shack and a greenhouse that teemed—not with plants—but with cats; beautiful, green-eyed, ghostly white cats.

A hermit of sorts lived there, and after he died, they tore down his buildings and removed the piles of accumulated junk. The wilderness did the rest, moving in and covering up the scars. We know the place well, having parked our car there often during the first year of our skiing. We would park our car and walk over and tap on the windows to entertain the cats before we pushed off on our skis. We recognize the old homestead now only by a peculiar dip in the road where we amateurs took a few spills on icy days. *What did they do with all the white cats?* we wonder.

Before we leave the park, we drive to the amphitheater parking lot, leave our car, and follow the forest trail to the meadow where we spread our coats on the deer-flattened grass and sprawl in the October sun. It is soothingly still— the only sounds are the susurration of the alder leaves and the infrequent mewing of the gulls wheeling high overhead.

Poquito reminds us that the sun is behind a cloud and that it's half a mile back to the car and fifteen miles from there to home, so let's get a move on. She knows that a few hours of hiking and basking, browsing and deer-watching are all that we can handle in one afternoon.

We don't take the back roads home; the highway is the

fastest route to the fridge and the easy chair and the evening news, so we join the line of tailgaters, and I grumble aloud as my sinuses are assailed by the exhaust fumes. Just where are all these people going, and why don't they take the back roads? Are they controlled by a herding instinct? Motivated by an insecurity that tells them there is safety only in the crowd? Is it an urban affliction? If so, when did Everett and I lose it? For lose it we certainly did.

Now, when we venture into Green Bay, or, perish the thought, Chicago, we find ourselves in the same panicky predicament as the little girl who grew up in treeless Nome, Alaska, and was taken to Seattle on a visit. She became hysterical while walking down an elm-lined street, afraid the trees were about to fall down on top of her.

We aren't intimidated by towering trees or buildings, but we do suffer a strange claustrophobia brought on by the crowds, the incessant traffic, and the noise. Does the urban tourist suffer that in reverse? Does he experience vertigo when he finds himself surrounded by nothing more substantial than hedgerows and cornfields? When there is nothing in his rearview mirror but an empty ribbon of road as far as the eye can see? I wouldn't be surprised.

Whatever the case, we're not complaining. We wouldn't trade our Hawthorn-Melody vistas and our close encounters with foxes and hares, hedgehogs and gophers, raccoons and deer for all the gift shops and restaurants between Sturgeon Bay and Gill's Rock.

When I was in high school I read Robert Frost's poem ''The Road Not Taken,'' a simple piece of four stanzas that tells of two roads that diverged in a wood, and the poet's decision to take the road ''less traveled by.'' That choice, he concluded, ''has made all the difference.'' I was quite impressed by the poem, even to the point of memorizing it; and decided I, too, would choose the less traveled road, although at that point in life I was not quite sure if I would recognize it when I came to it.

A year later I heard a minister speak somewhat more profoundly on the same topic of "a road less traveled." His text was not Frost's poem but Matthew's gospel, and the words were those of Christ. My scalp tingled and a frisson of awe ran through me as I heard for the first time: "Enter by the narrow gate; For the gate is wide, and the way is broad that leads to destruction, and many are those who enter by it. For the gate is small, and the way is narrow that leads to life, and few are those who find it."*

I desperately wanted to be one of those few, and that morning I answered the minister's invitation and went forward, accepting Christ as my Savior and Lord. And that *has* made all the difference! On this narrow, less-traveled road, I will not pretend that I have found it easier. Back roads never are. But I travel it with confidence because it is the right road, it leads me Home, and I know what it is to be lost on the highway.

*Matthew 7:13-14, NASB.

7

Tracking the Wild Thimbleberry

LAST FALL we took advantage of a bonus Indian Summer weekend, packed our bags, and took a senior sneak to rugged and beautiful Keewenaw country in Michigan's Upper Peninsula. It may have been November, but the sun was so warm, the air so invigorating, we decided to have a picnic lunch on the shores of Lake Fanny Hooe in Fort Wilkins State Park. We stopped at a grocery store in nearby Copper Harbor for the fixin's, and as we waited for our change, I spied a pyramid of home-made jams and jellies on the counter next to the cash register. Excitedly I pounced on one of the jars, a half-pint of preserves bearing the hand-written label "Thimbleberry Jam," and showed it to Everett.

"Do you realize that it was all of twenty-eight years ago and only a couple of miles from here that we discovered this treat?" I reminded him.

We had stopped at a roadside stand then where some overalled children were selling their mother's jams, jellies, and pickles. There, intrigued by the name "thimbleberry" and encouraged by the sales pitch of the aggressive youngsters, we had bought our first jar of the wild berry jam and found it to be as delicious as the tow-headed venders had

61

promised. It wasn't until some twenty years later that we were to taste it again — when we found it could be had for the picking in our Door County environs.

"Look at the price, will you!" I urged Everett, pointing to the $3.75 crayoned on the lid and anxious to impress upon him the value of the rare-as-rubies berry that we now pursue and take for granted each summer.

"Well, it's worth every penny!" he bristled, and I knew he was referring not so much to the taste as to the blood, sweat, and tears that had gone into its capture and production.

I returned the jar to the counter a bit reluctantly. I would have liked to buy it if only to encourage the enterprising farmwife, but since I had several like it on our shelves back home in Ellison Bay, I decided to leave it there for the next inquisitive tourist who might purchase the quaintly tagged jar out of curiosity and end up as we did, addicted to the delicacy.

What is a thimbleberry? Place a jar of thimbleberry jam next to one of wild raspberry and only an expert can tell the difference. Spread a little of each on a Swedish pancake, spear a forkful and place it on the tongue, and the one that titillates the tastebuds more tantilizingly is the thimbleberry.

The thimbleberry, in fact, is rather loosely related to the raspberry, and quite often where one is found the other grows nearby. They both appear to thrive alongside dusty roads, especially in what one of our neighbors calls "slashings," where trees have been felled to make way for new roads or power lines. They also flourish along abandoned lumber roads and right-of-ways. But whereas the tiny raspberry is bold and makes no secret of its whereabouts,

the outsized thimbleberry is shy and takes refuge behind and under the huge leaves of its bush.

The raspberry tends to be accommodating, growing in clusters so that one can stop and fill half a container from one healthy plant. The thimbleberry is less generous, and the picker has to keep on the move. One berry here, two over there, three beyond the next hummock — and look, isn't that another across the road? The raspberry says, "Here we are. Be our guest!" The thimbleberry prefers to play hide-and-go-seek.

When we first began searching for thimbleberries, it didn't help that we had no inkling as to what to look for or where. Rural folk are ordinarily quite helpful, but when it comes to disclosing their favorite hunting grounds or fishing holes, their charity never leaves home. Likewise with berries. One of my worst gaffes was to ask an old-timer, who had let it slip that he was anticipating a heavy crop of wild berries, where the best picking could be found. He raised an indignant eyebrow, turned a deaf ear, and changed the topic of conversation.

When I attacked from a different quarter and asked merely and humbly for a description of the plant (both our dictionary and encyclopedia had failed us) he remembered something he had forgotten to do and excused himself to join another circle of friends. I realize now, too late, that I might as well have asked our neighbor where he and his wife stashed the family jewels. And to tell the truth, now that we are living off the land as it were, Everett and I tend to be just as close-mouthed as the natives when it comes to our sources of supply.

Not that there isn't an occasional leak. Last year, our resident naturalist, Roy Lukes, spilled the beans in his weekly column in *The Advocate* by writing a paean to the thimbleberry, complete with photograph. As a result, the following weekend everyone and his city cousin were harvesting berries along the road from Bailey's Harbor to the Yacht Club. Fortunately, that particular stretch is not one of our favorite haunts — too public for our tastes — so we were not overly alarmed; but we pray that it was only an enthusiasm of the moment, a passing fancy that will not be revived. We hope Mr. Lukes will see the error of his ways and destroy that particular essay lest it be resurrected and immortalized in his next book.

When we stumbled across our first thimbleberry patch a few years ago, most of our summer social life was thenceforth committed. That was a great relief to Everett since it delivered him from having to pay for and sit through the summer symphonic concerts at Gibraltar. It also saved him the expense of taking me out to sample the new restaurants and gift shops that are proliferating all over the peninsula. And it spared him the therapeutic shopping expeditions to Green Bay.

Not that one can't combine berrying with any or all of the above. *One* can; but *I* can't. I find that as I age awkwardly I tend to be single-minded in my interests, that I seem to have arrived at the age and systolic range where I can sustain only one enthusiasm at a time; ergo, everything else in the months of July and August has to give way to thimbleberrying. Not only do we give the sport our total concentration, we have developed our own system and broken it down into two approaches: the casual and the fanatic.

The casual is a kind of browsing and is usually employed at the beginning and at the end of the season. In the middle of the afternoon, when Everett starts to nod over his newspaper; or in the early evening when the TV is all her-ringbone and static, a common summer syndrome, I suggest, "Let's go browse for berries." Since it's a cheap, spur-of-the-moment date, requiring no dressing up, my spouse is usually amenable. We go as we are. All the gear we need is already in the front seat of the car — boxes and repellent.

We take to the back roads, drive at a crawl, and scan the foliage along both sides. When I see a ripe berry, I gasp; it's purely reflexive and it alerts Everett, but he doesn't stop until my gasps and exclamations reach a certain pitch and frequency. He knows then that he'd better brake, reverse a few hundred feet, and pull off, for I have spotted a patch of ripening fruit. Actually, the pickings are slim on a browse; it may take us three trips to get enough fruit for a half pint of jam, but then I never said thimbleberrying was easy.

I have mixed emotions about the casual approach. I enjoy the fact that it's cleaner — we're traveling on paved roads, for one thing. The mosquitoes are fewer because the high-way crews keep the shoulders mowed, but I don't like the lack of privacy. I cannot shake the uncomfortable feeling that I am up to no good. I have the urbanite conviction that nothing in life is free, not even wild berries along a country road; so I tend to pick furtively, keeping my basket out of sight, snatching a berry here and there between passing cars, pretending to be bird-watching when a motorist slows down out of curiosity.

Everett laughs at my timidity. Boldly amoral in pursuits of this type, he is not put off by an audience. I have decided he is descended from a long line of poachers, and although he would never enter an orchard uninvited nor borrow an ear of corn from a neighbor's field, he ignores *No Trespassing*

66

signs that are posted on prairie lands and on the fringes of woodlands, helping himself freely to whatever grows wild and appeals to his palate.

When the thimbleberries are at their peak, we cease our road-combing and get down to business. I awaken one morning with a strong sense of destiny and announce to my husband and my dog that this is it, the day for which we have been rehearsing. I lure Everett out of bed with a hearty breakfast, say "Pshaw!" to his protestations, and set up the counter next to the stove with prophylactic precision against our return.

This time we dress for the occasion. Well, at any rate, I do. The woods are sure to be hot and humid, but they are also full of insects; so slacks and a long-sleeved jacket are required. I tie a scarf around my head for further protection, and I slather myself strategically with Cutter. (No matter what the commercials say about a drop here and there, slathering is a must.) I decide in favor of ankle-high, suede-finished hiking boots rather than gym shoes; and as an afterthought I grab a chilled can of soda from the re-frigerator. Dehydration will be a problem for me before the morning is over, muffled as I am in my sauna wear.

Everett has made no concessions; it is enough, he thinks, that he is accompanying me. He wears his rumpled cotton slacks and a three-day-old, short-sleeved, threadbare shirt, his costume du jour from June through September. I offer him the bottle of repellent, and he waves it away with a laugh.

"He jests at repellent," I remark aloud to Poquito, who sits between us on her padded pooch deck, "who never felt a bite!"

"I just follow the advice of an old Indian guide I once knew in the Pocono Mountains of Pennsylvania," Everett defends himself. "If white man want to survive in woods and elude mosquito and catchum thimbleberry, he must not shampoo or lather; he must not use shaving cream, Right Guard, or Bounce!"

I hold my peace, content that I have overcome his initial inertia, but wondering if I will ever be able to fathom the man, because although he would be the first to admit that there is nothing on this earth to compare with jam made from the fruit of the thimbleberry, and although he swears that a thimbleberry cream-cheese pie is gourmet fare, left alone he would postpone the foraging—and has indeed done so—until the crop is nearly gone. He surrenders to my pleas and proddings, but only under protest, along with the familiar declaration that this is the last time, *the very last time,* that he will go a-berrying. But once he is out in the field, with his nose to the ground, so to speak, a transformation takes place and he displays the maniacal zeal of our Chihuahua on the trail of a chipmunk. Whereas I try to stay within a short sprint from the car, in the event I am pursued by a wasp or a bear, Everett strikes out down the nearest thimbleberry trail, clambering over rotting logs and fallen trees, plunging through briar patches and muddy bogs, returning only when the lode or his legs give out—as though the whole idea was his in the first place.

Whenever we arrive at our destination, usually a gravel-covered, dead-end road, lined with dark woods and shoulder-high thimbleberry plants, we set to with a vengeance—Everett on one side of the lane and I on the other—with Poquito trotting back and forth between us trying to pick up a trail of her own to pursue. I remember to warn my husband to watch out for no trespassing signs and poison ivy, even though it's a vain admonition. The former he refuses to recognize, and the latter he can't.

He dives noisily into the underbrush, and I turn my back on him, step carefully into a berry patch and brace myself for my first eyeball to eyeball confrontation with the thimbleberry's guest, the harvestman. Time was when I recoiled with a scream; now I just blow gently at him and he relinquishes the plump, ripe berry, scrambling out of sight as fast as his octet of legs will carry him. The mosquitoes are not so easily discouraged; their sense of smell penetrates the aura of slathered Cutter; they are emboldened by the potpourri of Irish Spring and Incredible VO5 14-Hour Hold; intoxicated by Jean Naté talc and deodorant, and they make their first voracious passes at my hands, which reek of Lemon Joy from washing the breakfast dishes. There were, alas, no Indian guides in my background.

By the time I rejoin Everett at the car, I have more mosquito bites than berries, my scarf is askew, my spectacles have slid to the end of my nose, I am covered with nettles to my waist, my face is flushed an apoplectic purple, and I am itching furiously from head to sopping toes, convinced that I have picked up — along with the berries — at least one of the poison: oak, sumac, or ivy.

Everett, except for a few sticky spider webs trailing from his ears, returns unscathed, ready to move on to the next berry patch. We get into the car, turn on the air conditioner full blast, and drive on down the road a few hundred yards until we find another promising area. Feeling somewhat like a boxer between rounds, I finish guzzling my coke, blot the damp spots behind my ears and on my brow, retie my kerchief, and this time opt for a layer of OFF! before heading for the underbrush.

After an hour or so we pool our berries and find that the

hunt has yielded about a pint and a half. It seems a pitifully small return for all that effort and anguish, but cooked with a cup and a half of sugar it will produce three delectable, jewel-toned jars of jam. And four or five more weeks of early morning berrying expeditions, as the fruit continues to ripen, and we will have enough jam for our friends as well as for ourselves.

One evening last December we sat at our kitchen table, winds howling at the eaves, having an undeserved bedtime snack of homemade bread and thimbleberry jam and mugs of hot chocolate. Everett picked up the half-depleted jar of jam and held it to the light, turning it this way and that, the expression on his face quietly reflective.

"What are you doing?" I asked. "Comparing the agony of the chase with the ecstasy of the taste?"

He answered with a question of his own. "How much did this jar of jam cost us?"

I wasn't too sure about the price of sugar, but I hazarded a guess. "About ten cents. Maybe twenty, if you count the jar and the lid. Quite a bargain, isn't it?"

I knew what had triggered the question. We had been down to Bea's at Gill's Rock that afternoon to pick up some boxes of jams to send to the children for Christmas and had asked the friendly clerk to leave a space in each for a jar of our own thimbleberry jam.

"Thimbleberry?" She paused in her packing. "Why, that's worth its weight in gold! Do you know there was a man in here a few weeks ago asking for thimbleberry jam? He had been hunting high and low for a jar to take home with him. Hadn't had any since he was a kid. We didn't have any for sale, of course. It just wouldn't pay to put it up. But Bea told him she had some of her own at the house, and if he really wanted it — Do you know he offered her five dollars for that jar of jam — and was happy to get it at that price?''

Everett had been more quiet than usual as we drove home with our purchases. It seemed to me that he handled the gift jars of thimbleberry jam with added respect as he tucked them in amid the excelsior and prepared the boxes for mailing.

"Careful you don't drop it!'' I warned him that night as he admired the jar of jam he was holding to the light.

He grinned and set the glass down on the checkered cloth.

"You want to know what I'm thinking? That lady in the Upper Peninsula was making a profit of three fifty-five on each jar of jam she sold,'' he declared, looking at me speculatively. "And Bea made a whopping four dollars and eighty cents.''

I sensed what was coming next. A business proposition, impure and devious.

"Why, do you know,'' he continued, "we could average five dollars an hour at this?''

"Nothing doing,'' I said, getting up to clear the table.

He ignored my protest, warming to his vision of a clever hedge against inflation. "The Beach Road Market will sell them,'' he said confidently. "And the Pioneer Store.''

"Everett, forget it.''

"Of course, they'll want a cut; so I suppose that will knock down our profit somewhat, but it will still be a healthy one.''

As I rinsed the cups at the sink, I could see his reflection in the window before me. He was still cogitating, nodding his head in agreement with whatever it was he was consider-

71

ing. I thought I'd better puncture his balloon before he started designing labels reading "Reichel's Berry Farm." I took the jar of jam from his hand and returned it to the refrigerator.

"You don't like the idea, do you?" he asked.

"Frankly, no. There are some things I will do out of love that I will not do for money, and picking thimbleberries is one of them," I asserted, expecting a rebuttal.

"It's a tremendous idea," he began, and then he shrugged resignedly. "But I'm glad you're not interested. We're too old to start an ambitious project like that."

He fell asleep that night within seconds after hitting the pillow. I was not so lucky. The seed of the idea he had planted took root, sprouted, and sent out tentacles, and I lay awake until dawn computing overhead and profits and estimated berry yields. I finally succumbed to fatigue while counting jars of thimbleberry jam lined up on pantry shelves.

The next morning I pushed the homemade jam to the rear of the refrigerator and served Crosse and Blackwell marmalade with our French toast. *There are times that call for discretion,* I thought, and this was one of those times.

8

Required Eating

"The Door County Fish Boil is a fish steak dinner and a legend reaching mythical status in the Great Lakes area. This is so much a part of cult and culture that tourists from neighboring states make annual pilgrimages to Door County once they've participated . . . The "fish boil" has become not only a tradition but a gourmet's delight . . . a dramatic ceremony . . . enjoyed by those who claim they don't like fish and relished by all who love a good fish dinner."
(From the 1979 Door County Vacation Guide)

IT WAS A GENTLE, warm, spring afternoon, and having spent most of the day raking and bagging last year's leaves and birdseed husks, my spouse and I sprawled in our lawn chairs and exposed our arthritic joints to a little beneficent solar healing. Lazily we lay there and watched the honey bees — drop-ins from the cherry orchard down the road — assaulting our crocuses, and dreamily we listened to the contented twitterings of the finches as they preened themselves in the branches overhead.

"Beautiful!" I sighed. "God's in His heaven, and all the neighbors' kids are in school."

Everett grunted his agreement.

I raised my chair a notch to get a better view of the Eden

in which we were luxuriating. The narrow yard that surrounds our mobile home isn't exactly a corner of Biltmore Gardens; it has more the look of an abandoned victory plot, but it has come a long way in the seven years since we bought our first set of garden tools. Back then, in the first flush of rusticity, we had reasoned innocently that if the desert could be made to blossom like a rose, surely we could make our gravel and landfill do likewise. So we had brought with us from the city nurseries sprigs of clematis, mock orange, and forsythia, immature yews and adolescent arbor vitae; and while I stood by to advise and encourage, Everett excavated with pick and shovel.

Now, their roots embedded in the unfriendly shale, our plants were unaccountably thriving on a combination of fresh air, compliments, and an expensive blue liquid called Watch-Us-Grow. Tall and resplendent, they bloom in season; they provide shade as well as privacy, and they are a conversation piece that helps keep our visitors' minds and eyes off our lawn, which is a variegated carpet of thistles, dandelions, crabgrass, plantain, and bindweed. The lawn is a conversation piece of another sort and a contentious bone that I keep dragging out of the cupboard.

"I hate to keep dwelling on it," I apologized to Everett last fall, hoping I could persuade him to plow up the whole mess and begin again.

"Well, you're going to have to," he declared, turning my apology into a pun and striding off, adamant as ever, determined that his third unsuccessful attempt at lawn planting was his last.

But today was not a day to mull over negative thoughts, so I lifted my eyes from the lawn and up to the distant hills and the orchards that crowned them, and the neighboring

pasture where cattle were peacefully grazing. The bucolic landscape demanded a literary response, but, two years removed from the classroom, all I could recall were lines such as "The stag at eve had drunk his fill . . ." and "The curfew tolls the knell of parting day, and the lowing herd wind slowly o'er the lea." Neither of the verses seemed particularly relevant at three in the afternoon. I coaxed my sluggish memory, and finally a quotation from Solomon surfaced.

"The flowers appear on the earth!" I marveled. "The time of the singing of the birds is come, and —" I faltered for a moment and then, memory failing me again, I winged the conclusion. "And the sound of the scouring of the kettles is heard in the land."

Everett rolled his head lazily in my direction. "Just what is that supposed to mean?"

"It means if the crocuses are blooming, can the fish boils be far behind?"

He snorted. "You're rushing things. Fish boils are still a good two months away."

That may be, I thought, but while we were sitting there lazily "cultivating" our garden, the entrepreneurs of the over-sized soup pots were most likely girding and flexing and stock-piling in preparation for the first migratory wave of outlanders.

"We'd better enjoy this while we can," I warned my husband. "Before the invasion."

"They'll be swarming up here like lemmings to the sea," he agreed.

"Or like pilgrims to Canterbury," the English teacher in me contributed.

We watched an oriole tear apart an orange that we had nailed to a nearby stump. From a branch a few feet away, a second handsome male warbled, "Save some for me! Save some for me!"

Everett shook his head in consternation. "You know, there were four things Solomon couldn't fathom: 'the way of an eagle in the air, the way of a ship in the sea, the way of a serpent upon a rock, and the way of a man with a maid.'"

"And you would like to add a fifth mystery?" I ventured.

"You bet! The *why* of a crowd at a fish boil!"

"Ah, yes," I murmured, remembering. It would begin with phone calls, friends from Chicago and environs alerting us that they were on their way north, considerately giving us a "drop-in" time. They would tool up highway 42 in their gas-guzzlers; surrender a shah's ransom for a weekend stay in a roadside motel; spend most of their waking hours making the rounds of the potteries and quilteries and wineries, submitting their VISA platelets at each stop as though for validation before moving on to the next, counting it a moral defeat if they came out of any tourist trap empty-handed; they would mini-golf and go-cart and straddle tired nags on dusty bridle trails. All this, they tell us, in preparation for the gustatorial experience of topping off the evening at a fish boil.

I suppose part of the fascination that fish boils have for the tourists is the quaintness of the custom — a calculated and commercial quaintness that also offers lingonberries and Swedish pancakes for breakfast, meatballs and fruit soup for lunch at almost every restaurant north of the Sturgeon Bay bridge, and an ambience of bedragoned roofs and rosemaled shutters.

Or maybe it's not the quaintness at all; perhaps it's man's atavistic nature that draws him to the primitive scene: tattooed chefs tend huge caldrons filled with fish chunks,

77

potatoes, and onions. They dart in and out to feed the flames and keep the water at the boil, dramatically throwing kerosene on the log fire at the precise moment of doneness, which triggers the "overboil" that carries off the scum. Finally, brawny cook at either end, they lift the basket from the kettle with long poles and transport it to the serving tables. The whole performance is spurred on by the gasps and cheers from the waiting crowds, highlighted by the flickering flames and the popping of flashbulbs. For a few moments they have been transported back in time to Eric the Red and the Viking victory feasts after the pillaging of some coastal village. Anyway, that's the way I've heard some folks tell it, but I possess an imagination that is a bit warped and tends to veer in a different direction geographically and time-wise.

"Reminds me," I whispered to Everett my first time around, "of the jungles of New Guinea and *missionaire du jour!*"

The fact of the matter is that we are not fish eaters. Everett has never advanced beyond oysters and sees no need to, whereas a fish dinner to me is a can of Sockeye skillfully disguised beyond recognition in a loafpan or casserole, as far removed from the briny as I can take it.

Not that we have never given fish boils a chance. On the contrary, we have given them three chances. "That's above and beyond the call," my husband avows. We attended our first fish boil out of curiosity, along with the universal compulsion to get in line. Surely, we thought — anyone would think it — that a meal that would attract such long queues of happy, salivating vacationers must be worth the price and the patience. We came away disillusioned, rationalizing our failure to smack our lips over boiled whitefish by reminding ourselves that the Japanese enjoy squid and the French snails, and it was quite possible that one must have a Scandinavian palate in order to enjoy a fish boil.

We gave it a second shot the following summer, dressed for the occasion in our new hand-knit Norwegian sweaters, accompanied by tourist friends invited for the sake of conviviality, and anointed at the wrists and behind the ears with Cutter, the eau de cologne of the North Woods. We put on a brave act, but we didn't fool our guests, lobster and oyster folk from the East Coast. They wholeheartedly endorsed our subsequent purchase of several Deluxe Celeste pizzas to round off the evening.

We tried to pass up the third fish boil by painstakingly describing it to our daughter and son-in-law who were impatient to partake.

"It's a monochromatic meal," I warned them, hoping to alert their aesthetic sensibilities. At the same time I removed from the fridge a beautifully garnished bowl of my best potato salad and set it on the kitchen table, hoping to tempt them beyond their endurance.

"*A*-chromatic," Everett corrected me. "White. Everything's white."

They were not put off. They tore their eyes away from the radish roses and the paprika-dusted egg slices, rose from their chairs, and headed for the door.

"The fish is white," I emphasized. "A blanched, anemic white —"

"Toad-belly white," added Everett, who desperately preferred to stay home and feast on cheeseburgers and potato salad, and who was still clinging to the arms of his chair.

"The boiled potatoes are white, and so are the onions," I added unnecessarily, getting out the grill for the hamburger patties.

79

"And they roll around on a white cardboard plate, and you spear them with white plastic forks," Everett embellished, handing me a cutting board and a large Bermuda.

"The cole slaw is white, too. Isn't it, dear?"

"Well, yes, a sort of greeny white; but white, nevertheless."

"And then there's the bread—" I began, knowing in advance my husband's reaction.

"Storebread!" He sputtered, backing out of the refrigerator where he had been searching for the sliced cheese. "Fresh from its Wondercup wrapper! White bread, limp, no character at all!"

"At our last fish boil your father took his bread and rolled it into pellets and threw it to the starlings at our table." I felt it was only fair to warn the children.

"*At* them — not *to* them!"

"Of course, there is brown bread, too — limpa — if you don't mind your bread tasting like anise."

It was evident we were not making any headway with these young people who had dined on moose and ptarmigan in Indian camps in northern Quebec, and who had also drooled over squirrels and lizards while in survival training in central Mexico. But I decided to make one last, low stab at dissuasion.

"The only real contrast in this white-on-white meal is provided by the flies," I cautioned. "Hordes of them, ecstatically drunk, wheeling, flying, staggering from fish to potatoes to slaw, some of them riding the fork all the way to its destination; some of them preferring to sate themselves entirely on your slab of cherry pie —"

"Cherry pie?" my son-in-law interrupted. "What are we waiting for? Let's get going before they run out of dessert!"

Well, the kids were paying, so we had no choice but to follow. However, if I had known that a cherry pie could tip the scales, I would have baked a half dozen.

It was after that third fish boil that we determined that the next time visiting kith or kin expressed an interest in this quaint Scandinavian picnic, we would give them directions, the keys to the car, a fly swatter, and our blessing. After which, we would wave good-bye and retreat indoors to scramble a few eggs.

"Shame on you!" says one native after another when we confess our antipathy toward fish boils. But whatever smidgen of guilt or disloyalty we felt disappeared when we met an undiluted Norwegian, a highly-respected, lifelong resident of North Bay, who admits to not caring for fish in any way, shape, or kettle.

"If all of us fish boil dissenters were lined up end to end in Door County—" I began, stopping to wave away the bees with whom I had developed an *entente cordiale* over the past hour.

"We'd be stomped to death by the hungry mobs rushing to get in line for the nearest boil," Everett concluded.

He's right. We're a minority, and our combined huffing and puffing could not snuff out one fire under one caldron of simmering fish and potatoes. Not that we would try. The boils are proliferating at an alarming rate. Whether it be under ecclesiastical sponsorship, in the parking lot of the local Lutheran congregation; or civic-supported, in the town square; or just run by the local restauranteur cashing in— somewhere from Sturgeon Bay north to Washington Island, through the months of June, July, and August and a few weekends after that—there will be umpteen pots of fish cooking over open fires, and thousands of voracious, sunburned patrons queued up at each. And if you're a do-it-yourselfer, you can rent your own caldron at Nelson's Hardware in Bailey's Harbor!

"Everett, I agree. It *is* a mystery. The closest I can come to empathy is when I recall the nigh unbearable craving that overwhelms me every now and then for a corned beef on rye from Link's Deli on Addison Street back in Chicago. For that, I would travel two hundred eighty miles. On foot.

"You know, I think I'll do an article on fish boils."

"Go on record?" Everett questioned. "If you write it up and it gets into print, you're going to be in trouble with a lot of Scandinavians!"

"It won't be the first time. I'll just follow the example of my English forebears when *they* were being harrassed by the Vikings."

"What's that?"

"I'll recite the prayer they used to pray: 'God, deliver us from the fury of the marauders of the North!' "

9

The Conversation Piece

I HAVE JUST ORDERED my husband's Christmas present. It's a sweatshirt — a personalized one.

I sent away to a place in Colorado that advertises in the back pages of one of my monthly magazines: "We print any message you want." What I wanted — and I made it quite explicit in my order — were two separate quotations on one shirt. Across the front I directed them to emblazon: I'M WAITING FOR THE GLUE TO DRY, and on the back: I'LL BE OUT IN THE BARN. These are not provocative profundities that I lifted from *Bartlett's Familiar Quotations* or swiped from somebody's bumper sticker. They just happen to be memorable words around our house and deserve to be preserved, if only because they pretty much represent the total of Everett's working vocabulary since our retirement.

In the likely event that my husband's vocal chords should ever atrophy through lack of exercise, he will have reason to appreciate my foresight. By merely pointing either to his chest or to his shoulder blades, he will be able to keep open our channels of communication. Providing he is wearing his sweatshirt. And he will be — once he tries it on for size at Christmas he is not apt to take it off until spring thaw.

Conversation in our household began to deteriorate when our four children grew up and went their separate ways. By the time my husband and I had fled the city and settled here in what I was sure would be Beulah Land, dialogue had preceded us in death, and we were surrounded by silence — a silence broken only by the clicking of the dog's toenails on the kitchen linoleum and the occasional humming of the refrigerator. There are those who call it a "companionable silence" — this ultimate intimacy that results from thirty-some years of marriage to the same spouse. Everett is of that persuasion. He believes that there's a peculiar kind of ESP between long-wedded folk that makes verbal exchanges almost unnecessary. I, on the other hand, have developed a tremendous sympathy for the loneliness of the long-distance runner.

There is something to be said for taciturnity, I suppose. Not much, naturally; but something. Especially in the dawn's early light. Our monotonous dieter's breakfast of poached egg, unbuttered toast, and orange juice does not require comment; and once we have put out the pup, checked the vacillations of the barometer and the level of the thermometer, measured the rain gauge or the depth of the snow on the bird bath, conversation — the primal grunts and groans of it — comes to a halt.

At 8 A.M., after we have sat through the local news, from a barn fire in Forestville to the Peterson Pool schedule in Sturgeon Bay, I retreat to my typewriter while Everett does the dishes, after his fashion. A few minutes before nine, he pauses at my door long enough to utter his first full intelligible sentence of the day: "I'll be out in the barn," he tells me.

Some days there are variations on that original theme

84

when he will, in a downright garrulous mood, expand and comment: "Well, I'll be out in the barn." My imagination seizes on that "Well." I see it as an important prefatory, implying that he is in one of his more cooperative moods, and that if for any reason I need his help, I know where to find him. That "Well" could even suggest that if there are any errands to run, and I can think of them quickly enough, he will take care of them first, before he applies himself to lathe and drill. It even suggests to my imaginative mind that there is a bit of reluctance on his part at leaving me. I like that interpretation best, but I don't pursue the projection. We both have deadlines to meet — I at my typewriter, and he at his workbench.

Several times during the morning he returns to the house, and I look at him expectantly as he passes my study doorway. A package from United Parcel? A sliver to be removed? A rare bird at the feeders? None of these. It's always a laconic, "I'm waiting for the glue to dry." Then he and our Chihuahua settle into their favorite chair for a good read or a snooze until the glue has indeed hardened. Then, "I'll be out in the barn," he reports, slipping into his jacket and out of the house.

By noon I am starving for both food and conversation. "Is there any mail?" I ask as I set the table. This question merits, no matter what the postman may have delivered, a cryptic "Not much." "Not much" is one of Everett's favorite phrases, and he employs it often. Different inflections, I'll grant you, but the same two words.

I set before him a Swiss cheese on rye and pour his glass of 2% milk.

"What did you accomplish this morning?" I ask in a second attempt to get a conversation going.

"Not much," he confides, slipping a tidbit to Poquito.

I wait for an elaboration and when there is none, I try again.

"Didn't I hear you talking to the oil man?"

Half a grunt and nod while he pours a few drops of milk into a saucer for Poquito is all the reply I receive.

"Did he have anything to say?" I pursue relentlessly.

This time he waxes eloquent. "Oh, not much."

I sigh and retire to my sandwich, spending the rest of our lunch break looking out the window, watching the pine siskins and gold finches and evening grosbeaks at their mid-day meal—all of them chattering a blue streak.

Everett and the dog finish first and move to the living room to read the newspaper.

"Anything interesting?" I ask hopefully, wandering in after clearing the table and straightening up the kitchen.

"Not much," he responds, handing me the paper in case I want to challenge his assessment.

Forty winks later he brushes the pup from his lap, heaves himself out of the chair and announces, "I'll be out in the barn."

I get out my quilting materials, turn on the radio, and listen gratefully to pesticide reports from the farm bureau, DNR debates from the state capital, and dire news from Yemen while I sew a fine seam and look for Everett to return with the news that he's "waiting for the glue to dry."

My husband says that there is something in the nature of most females that abhors a conversational vacuum, that attempts to fill every pause with inconsequential chit-chat. He cites me as a prime example and has even gone so far as to imply that eighteen years of holding forth in public school classrooms has sharpened and developed my natural propensity for small talk to the status of a talent. Naturally I disagree, but I will admit that when I resigned from teaching, the sudden transition from seven hours a day of non-stop academic dialoguing to a kind of connubial Coventry was a shock for which I was not prepared.

As a matter of fact, I had been impatient for retirement. I could hardly wait until our children were launched on their careers and Everett and I could head for the hills. I anticipated long lazy winter evenings before the blazing hearth during which we would exchange confidences, share ideas, and make new discoveries about each other; we would spend the autumn years playing "catch-up."

Alas, our hearth never materialized, and neither of us can quite make it to the ten o'clock news.

I looked forward to long hikes through spring-fresh woods, waxing Emersonian at each new toadstool and curly frond along the trail. But the hikes we take are studies in stamina, not nature walks, with Everett intent on "getting it over with" in a five-mile-per-hour lope, while I pant and struggle to keep him in sight.

I visualized hours of basking on deserted October beaches, contemplating the inexorable waves, spouting a few appropriate lines from Shakesperian sonnets, declaiming over the sounds of wind and surf: "Like as the waves make towards the pebbled shore, So do our minutes hasten to their end." But an unexpected irony in our dotage is that Everett's thermostat is malfunctioning, and sprawling on the sand leaves him cold, literally and figuratively; and his only comment on Shakespeare's similes is uttered through chattering teeth: "*My* end will come sooner than you think if we don't get back to the car and turn on the heater!"

It was Robert Browning who set me up. He and his

"Grow old along with me! The best is yet to be —" For Robert and Liz it probably was. In their cozy Italian palazzo they spent their mornings busily composing, and their candlelit evenings mutually admiring each other's sonnets. That kind of togetherness beats viewing *Little House on the Prairie* with a bowl of buttered Redenbacher's on one's lap.

"You should have married a poet," Everett sympathizes. There have been times in our long career, usually when he is on his way to the stereo to turn off a Rachmaninoff prelude, when he has told me I should have married a musician. And the day he discovered my shopping bags full of clippings from the Sunday travel sections of the *Tribune* — articles on places to go, stay, or avoid, from Greenland to New Zealand — he suggested I might have been happier married to a travel editor. He has told me also and often, for various and sundry reasons, that I should have latched on to a millionaire. Nowadays, when we meet that rare bird, a compulsive talker of the male gender, Everett will pull me to one side and say, "Now, there's the guy you should have married!"

The fact of the matter is, I *did* marry a garrulous guy. I can remember as though it were yesterday a Sunday morning on a Halsted Street trolley. We were newly-engaged, on our way to church, sitting on the long seat in the back. Everett interrupted his monologue to say, "You know, one of the reasons I love you is that you're such a good listener!"

I'm glad I was. Ninety percent of what I know about my mate is information gleaned by listening during our six-month engagement and the first year of our marriage. After that the children started coming, and as their powers of speech burgeoned, Everett's diminished. It didn't help matters that about the time the youngsters were branching out, I began an exciting adventure as a high school English teacher.

If my husband had wanted to make up for lost time, or even to pick up where he had left off twenty years before, he wouldn't have had a chance. Now it was I who needed a good listener, and he became my shoulder to cry on, my grievance committee, my safety valve. He listened — at least he assumed the posture — while I aired my many frustrations and crowed over my infrequent triumphs. For eighteen years he listened. No wonder he lost his desire to communicate.

I counted on his recovering his powers of speech in our retirement retreat. He didn't. I gave the matter serious thought, diagnosed his condition as *apatheia senilis* and prescribed a plethora of new activities. I nagged him into joining a men's prayer breakfast, an evening woodworking class, a Bible study kaffeeklatsch, and even a part-time job. My efforts at rehab came to naught. His taciturnity was too firmly established.

When I asked him one Tuesday morning after his return from The Viking what he had eaten, I received for an answer the standard and noncommittal: "The usual."

"What did you fellows talk about?"

"Not much."

"Who all were there?" I questioned, testing his memory.

"The same old bunch," he side-stepped neatly.

On Monday nights, on his return from Woodshop, I would brush the sawdust from his clothes and ask, "What did you do tonight?"

"Not much."

"Oh, come on!" I would jolly him along through

clenched teeth. "You must have done *something*!"

He'd reflect for a moment. "Hammered and sawed. Sawed and hammered."

Even his daily trips to the grocery store, a folksy emporium two miles down the road, and a clearing house for operations, accidents, and the latest bear stories, contribute nothing to the conversation at our board.

Nor does the barber shop. "Any news from town?" I still inquire hopefully when he comes home with a new haircut.

"Nope," he replies.

"Nope?" What kind of an answer is that? Why, a one-hour session at the beauty parlor would provide me with enough material for a full page in *The Door County Advocate*. And that's unprovoked, unsolicited, gratuitous gossip, garnered merely by keeping one ear out of the hair dryer!

One evening Everett and I sat across the room from each other, both of us deeply immersed in our books. I looked up for a moment to rest my eyes and became aware of the suffocating silence around us. The only sounds for the last hour had been the turning of the pages, the ticking of the cuckoo clock and the quarter-hour shenanigans of the dancers in the Black Forest timepiece. I sat there, lonely and longing for dialogue. I would have settled for an argument; nay, I would have welcomed a spat. If looks alone could have done it, my resentful glances at my complacent mate would have triggered at least a friendly debate.

Suddenly the phone rang, and I dashed eagerly across the room to answer. It was a bright young woman from the *Milwaukee Sentinel* calling to ask my opinion about everything from Three Mile Island to the presidential candidates to who's responsible for the oil crisis. My, what a good time I had! It ended all too soon to satisfy me.

"That was fun!" I exclaimed after replacing the receiver. "A telephone survey, eh? She really struck paydirt, didn't she?"

"Just what is that supposed to mean?"

He chuckled, not unkindly. "She must have thought you'd just been inoculated with a phonograph needle!"

Well, I had heard that chestnut before, so I let it pass. At least until I could work up a worthy rejoinder. Finally, I cleared my throat. I had a statement to make.

"I believe I know why they call the declining years 'The Golden Age,' " I said dryly. "It's because they're so silent."

Everett looked up at me uncomprehendingly.

"*You* know," I prompted. " 'Silence is Golden.' "

He grunted, unimpressed, and returned to his book.

"It should be 'Silence Is Olden.' " I persisted, aiming for a vulnerable spot.

He thought it over. I waited patiently for his answer.

" 'Silence Is Wisdom' is better still," he finally offered, clinching it with a biblical quote. " 'He that hath knowledge spareth his words.' "

"Olden," I muttered obstinately. " 'Silence is Olden.' "

"If you're implying that anyone around here is getting old — well, speak for yourself!"

Or had he said "Speak *to* yourself?" because he immediately withdrew from the debate, burrowing deeper into his armchair to resume his reading.

Well, I do that a lot — speak to myself. To myself and the dog and the *Saintpaulia ionanthas* in the living room and the gerania on the kitchen windowsill; to the chickadees lined up on my porch railing and to the squirrels after my crocuses. Teetering on the brink of non compos mentis, I am.

Well, that was the night I decided to order another item from the same company that inscribes sweat shirts. They also do bumper stickers. I printed the message I had in mind, made out a check, addressed, sealed, and stamped the envelope, and, with Poquito at my heels, ambled down to the mailbox to leave it there for the morning pick-up.

Everett might not be too happy about driving around town in a car that asks impertinently via bumper sticker: HAVE YOU SPOKEN TO YOUR WIFE TODAY? but even if the question serves only as a conversation piece, it will be worth it, I figure.

10

Tucker

No collection of stories, unless it is one about canines, should contain more than one chapter on dogs. It is difficult to imagine, but there are people out there who prefer cats, snakes, or even guppies to dogs. My own passion for dogs is not inherited—unless it skipped a generation, and my parents are the ones who lost out. I was permitted as a child to encourage cats to follow me home, but never dogs. Too bad, because my childhood was a lonely and unhappy one, and if ever a child needed the therapy of a dog to hug and cherish, it was I. I haven't outgrown my loneliness, nor my need for the unconditional love and selfless devotion of a dog. That is a point I had to make before I wrote about Tucker, a dog after my own heart.

AT 5:30 IN THE MORNING when the alarm clock, positioned halfway across the room the night before, jars me out of a sound sleep, reminding me that I have a rendezvous to keep, my Epicurean body wages a fierce resistance against my Spartan mind. Before Tucker entered my life, matter used to win most of the battles, and I would silence the strident nagging of the alarm and return to my cozy, quilted coccoon to arise at a more civilized hour—or whenever Everett called me for breakfast.

95

But now that I have a commitment of sorts — an early morning date with a dog — I make the supreme effort and navigate stiffly and drunkenly to the dresser, turn off the vibrating extension of my conscience, raise the window shades, and recoil from the sunshine creeping over the apple orchard and insinuating its way into my bedroom. I grope for my specs and my watch, stumble into the bathroom, splash water over my puffy phizzog, shudder at the specter in the mirror, run a brush through my hair to remove most of the tangles, struggle into my jogging slacks — a pair of bell-bottomed polyesters held up by sprung elastic and a couple of safety pins — and wriggle into a faded sweat shirt that declares in some runic language across its back: "Bicycling is good for the heart."

With no small measure of reluctance I leave my unconscious husband behind, hugging his pillow determinedly. I cast a resentful glance at Poquito, buried deep in layers of old sweaters, feigning sleep, but with one eye peering out of the depths, fearful I might take her with me. I down my four ounces of orange juice lest I fall along the wayside for lack of potassium, and I am off.

My course takes me up out of our wooded hollow and across the deserted highway where only two minutes from my back door I am already winded. I stop to catch my breath — and to wait for Tucker. I can never tell from which direction he will bound; it will depend on where he has spent the night. Sometimes he sneaks up from behind and I know he has enjoyed the hospitality of the Anderson farm; other mornings he will come crashing through the underbrush in the old Roen orchard, and I can assume then that he has slept at the Landstroms or the Hilanders; and often he will come rollicking down the driveway on the Swansons'

acres. No matter from which quarter, he always manages to surprise me, and the lovable tramp is well aware. Some mornings he doesn't show at all, and I continue on my constitutional alone, cast down, and wishing I had stayed in bed — and then halfway to my destination, the junction of Old Stage and Highview, I hear his heavy panting as he races to overtake me.

"Sorry," he apologizes, butting me gently with his enormous head, waiting for his hug and a vigorous ear-scratching. "Sorry, but I overslept."

Maybe his occasional tardiness is accidental; maybe not. I'm inclined to think he enjoys the extra caress and the outpourings of sweet nothings that gush forth when he shows up "after all." I wouldn't put it past him. He doesn't let me overdo it, however; with Tucker a little sentimentality goes a long way. At the precise point when enough is enough, he pulls away, impatient to get on with our walk.

We are not a well-matched team, Tucker and I, even though we both are carrying a lot of flab. Tucker's pace is a fluid, rippling trot; mine is a determined, arrhythmic lope that is a result of arthritic arches, rheumatic knees, and a sedentary life-style. He could run circles around me; could, but he is too much the gentleman to do so. Instead, he makes frequent sorties into the roadside weeds, allowing me to forge ahead. When he finds me lagging, he turns back, smiles at me with an encouraging "Aren't we having fun?" toss of his mane, and marks time until we are again abreast.

The road we travel is lined with cherry orchards on the south and hardwood forests on the north; wildflowers in season border both sides: butter-and-eggs, paintbrush, Queen Anne's lace, and chickory, my favorite. I pay more attention to the flora now that the wildlife is gone. This is the road on which I once encountered skunks and foxes and deer—even a runaway dam and her colt, but in the past year the forest has fallen prey to developers, and Tucker and I don't look for more than wooly brown caterpillars and flattened shrews.

Several sideroads have been bulldozed into the cool dark woods; the well-diggers are at work; and the cinderblock foundation of one house is already completed. Soon a row of ranch houses will profane the cleared areas, and for sale signs will be posted; and people who would never before have considered violating these woods will be tempted and succumb. Motorcycles and snowmobiles and plastic-draped motorboats will line their driveways, and there will be a proliferation of traffic from city relatives.

I try not to dwell on the tragedy of it—it's counter-productive. After all, I'm not here to lower my blood pressure, not raise it. But when I pass the spot where they chopped down "my" apple tree to make way for a drive-way, I nearly weep. Everett, who tends to accept life's vicis-situdes with the equanimity of a saint, comes close to tears, too. The fruit from that tree went into "his" apple pies.

Tucker isn't disturbed by insidious progress. Why should he be? Professional gentleman tramp that he is, he will benefit from it. He makes almost as many stops as the postman hereabouts and is just as welcome.

When we reach the half-mile point, Tucker resists the temptation to go on up the hill and visit the feisty little border collie that resides there behind the lilac hedge. He knows this is where I turn around and head back, so he does likewise. I do not flatter myself that Tucker's attachment is based on an instinctive appreciation of my sterling charac-ter. He just happens to know that if he sees me to my door after our walk is over, he will get his hors d'oeuvres: a couple of slices of Braunschweiger or a frankfurter. To his credit I must add that there are many mornings when he doesn't walk me all the way home, when other loyalties transcend his hunger and he parts company with me at the entrance to our court.

I suppose because Tucker finds it so easy to outwalk me he thought I would be no great challenge on my bike. He took me on one day when I was starting out on a five-mile cycle trek, and although I pedaled slowly and even stopped often so that he could catch up, it was an ordeal for him. It was a hot afternoon, and in spite of the fact I had chosen the easiest five miles in our vicinity, there were a fair number of hills. I could shift to low and climb them easily; Tucker slowed down, increased his panting, and labored up each rise. Once I tried to send him home. "Go home, Tucker!" I said sternly, stamping my foot to show I meant business. He flopped at my feet, tongue lolling and dripping, eyes half-closed. I said it again, even more forcefully: "Tucker, go home!" He looked up at me and smiled. "Go home? Where's home? Home is where the heart is."

I was a quarter-mile ahead of him when I reached my turn-around point, where Lakeview and Z meet on a windswept hill. I got off my Motobecane and sat in the grass under the shade tree and watched, agonizing, while Tucker struggled up the last long incline and collapsed wearily alongside me in the shade. I fished the ice cubes out of my thermos of orange juice and gave them to him to crunch. He didn't want to be petted; he was too hot. As soon as his heavily-coated body warmed the grassy patch on which he lay he would move to a cooler spot, but always staying within a few feet of where I sat.

100

We rested there a good long while; it is a tranquil place, hills undulating down to the open lake; cattle grazing in the meadows; larks and goldfinches providing a musical backdrop. I began to talk to Tucker. He has always loved that — to be told what a handsome creature he is, what a brave and stalwart and faithful dog. His eyes squinted in ecstasy while I rambled on enumerating his virtues, until he could stand it no longer, and half-rising, pulled himself across the few inches of grass separating us and laid his head in my lap.

When I finally started back, I traveled at full speed, hoping that Tucker, unable to keep up, would drop behind and visit some of his friends along the way. I pedaled furiously, and the first time I looked back he was running heavily and determinedly behind but losing ground. I shifted into high gear, certain I would get so far ahead he would lose interest in the chase. Positive I had left him loitering a couple of miles back, I turned around anyway — and there he was, a hundred yards behind me, limping but undaunted.

Since then, whenever he sees me on my bike, he escorts me a few yards down the road, just until I have time to make much of his presence; and then he resumes whatever it was he has been doing. He has never again tried drag-racing with me. Age isn't his nemesis; he is just too well fed and too soft.

Poquito, one-twentieth the size of Tucker, is two pounds overweight herself. She is also either near-sighted or foolhardy and she will attack cows, horses, Great Danes — from a distance, to be sure, but even up close, if they are inclined to take her seriously. When they first met, Tucker saw right through her bravado and treated her with good-humored deference, being careful not to crush her underfoot, ignoring her hysterical barking, and standing patiently still while she inspected him from tip to tail.

When Tucker occupies our small back porch, there is not enough clearance for Poquito. At least, that's what Poquito thinks. Actually, a dozen Chihuahuas could squeeze past Tucker and not come within flea's length. The first time that we opened the door to let Poquito out and she saw this behemoth sprawled there on the porch, she refused to leave the house. Tucker, sizing up the situation immediately, and gentleman that he is, rose, pressed himself as flat as possible against the railing to give her all the room she thought she needed to get past him and down into the yard. I am sure he did it with tongue in cheek. It was a graceful maneuver that he still performs.

Tucker has a canine friend down the road apiece; a nasty-dispositioned, bike-chasing boxer. I don't know if this raucous animal is interested in hamstringing me or just in shaking me up, but I wobble a lot when I pedal past his domain, and I pour on the speed to outdistance the salivating beast.

One morning Tucker was visiting his aggressive buddy when I came puffing up the road on my way back from the Beach Road Market. The boxer, fangs bared, streaked out of his yard barking and slavering. Alongside ran Tucker, every bit as eager, but a contrast in temperament. He was smiling his happy smile, waving his tangled tail, quite happy to see me — and I think quite pleased to have me see him in the company of another dog. However, his approach was so roundabout, I wondered for a moment if he were going to join in the attack, if only just for fun.

I couldn't have been more mistaken. He was running interference, keeping himself between his attacking play-

102

mate and me. When the boxer got within biting distance, Tucker swung around and with his body pressed against my legs, he shepherded me away from the combat zone, escorting me up the rest of the hill to the gravel driveway into our woods, where he sat, grinning perhaps at his adroitness, permitting me to pet him and tell him what a dear friend he was.

It was a most diplomatic gesture. He had protected me without alienating his pal. It is also typical of Tucker who had learned early in life that having the size and appearance of a young lion enabled him to take the discreet approach to valor.

Tucker is really a man's dog. When my husband is on the premises, Tucker will follow him companionably from barn to house, from mowing to painting, just for the pleasure of his company — certainly not for conversation. On the other hand I have had to work at developing our relationship, stooping to the art of conditioning with tasty handouts and a lot of sweet talk. I often have the feeling that he accepts my company only when there is nothing better to do. Everett says "Pshaw" to that; says I accuse *him* of the same thing.

One warm summer afternoon Everett and I sprawled in our lawn chairs soaking up the sunshine; Tucker lay nearby in the shade, watching us out of eyes half-closed in contentment. All at once, he rose and we assumed he was taking off for a visit with one of his other families, but that wasn't his intention at all. He settled on his haunches next to Everett's chair and gently laid his head on my husband's arm. We were accustomed to impulsive, affectionate outbursts from our Chihuahua, who's a real kissing bug, but not from Tucker. Now he had accepted us both.

We know nothing about Tucker's origins. The legend

around our part of Door County is that he was abandoned by some vacationers. I suppose it is true, but we find it difficult to believe that anyone having known him could throw him out of a car or lock him out of a summer cottage. As far as we know, he is persona grata on every doorstep for miles around; the senior citizens save their porkchop bones and chicken scraps for him after their luncheons; someone tackles him occasionally and gives him a good grooming. But who taught him his impeccable manners? After whom does he model his gallant behavior? Where did he learn to seek out those places where he is needed? To stay away when he is not wanted? To go through life with such equanimity, such a happy smile?

We don't know the answer. All we know is that one fall day I opened the door to step out into the back yard and there, a few feet from our stoop, sat a huge dog with a leonine head and a mane all tangled with burrs. His thick copper and white coat glistened in the sun, and his dark amber eyes brimmed over with good will. He sat there smiling and wagging his plume of a tail, a mixture of malamute and mystery, a magnificent dog. I waited for some indication from him as to the nature of his business, but he kept a discreet and deferential distance, leaving the overtures to me.

"Hello, there," I said. "And who are you?"

At the sound of my voice his smile broadened and the tempo of his tail increased. Rising, he made his way over to the porch, neither groveling nor overwhelming, but with dignity, presenting himself for inspection. There was a cloud of gnats around his head; he was sorely in need of currying; and I was sure he carried a heavy freight of fleas and tics, but none of those mattered in the presence of his quiet charisma. It was head over heels for me the minute I looked into his eyes. I hugged him gently and called to Everett, "Look what we have here!" My husband came and saw and was likewise overcome.

Tucker stayed for about a half hour on his first visit, permitting us to pet and fondle and feed him; but then he made it clear, with just the proper amount of reluctance, that he had other responsibilities and had to move on. But he returned the next day and every day after that for almost two years, becoming a close friend.

One day Tucker stopped coming. We missed him. We made inquiries. No one seemed to know his whereabouts. And then, a few weeks later, while we sat on a crowded bench in the vet's waiting room, an irate neighbor told us what had happened.

It appeared, he said, that Tucker must have misjudged someone's character; must have wagged his tail and smiled his endearing smile at the wrong person; visited the wrong doorstep. It had to have been a summer visitor, frightened by Tucker's friendly advances, or a dog-hater by nature, who called in a deputy and insisted Tucker be disposed of. Only a stranger to these parts could have been responsible. Only a summer deputy could have pulled the trigger. No native between Sister Bay and Newport, Tucker's itinerary, would have been able to lift a hand against the familiar, free-hearted wanderer.

Tucker never had the opportunity to be a heroic dog; not a Barry, dog of the Alps, rescuing avalanche victims; nor a Gelert, saving his master's child; nevertheless, he was the kind of dog, unpedigreed, undistinguished, and unremarkable, that writers have eulogized through the ages. No epitaph fits him more aptly than that written by a Newfoundland fisherman for his faithful companion:

". . . one who possessed Beauty without Vanity,
  Strength without Insolence,
    Courage without Ferocity,
      and all the virtues of Man without his Vices . . .
        a tribute to the Memory of [Tucker], a Dog."

11

The Night They Moved
the Medical Center

WE BROUGHT ALONG some old cushions to sit on, an afghan
for warmth, and a bottle of repellent for protection. If I
could find anything positive to say about this middle-of-
the-night escapade, it was that it was a good night for moving a building. The weather was mild and there was a fresh
breeze off the lake. The insects were few, and that was
fortunate for us, because Everett, who has been conditioned
to reach for his driver's license at the first flicker of a
flashing light, became so excited at seeing the road block-
aded by a police car with a revolving dome light, that he left
the OFF! and the afghan behind in the car.

Poquito had also been left behind, although she would
have loved sharing the thrill of a night on the town. However, I have made it a point to leave her home from most
public events ever since the day of the bicycle race in Ephraim when Everett, in order to snap a picture of the winning
cyclists straining into the final stretch, set Poquito down
near the finish line — and she spotted a handsome French
poodle across the road.

The actual moving date of the medical center building
had been postponed several times; and hope repeatedly de-

107

ferred had made my husband more eager and anxious than ever. He had gone to bed early, setting his alarm for 12:30, even though he knew I would be up and around reading or working a diacrostic. I had promised to awaken him, but his trust in me was not exactly implicit. When he went to bed, a patch of fog was hanging over the area, and he knew that if it thickened in the interim, I would be liable to take a pass on the night's adventure. It was his opinion that I was sufficiently stony-hearted to let him sleep through the whole brouhaha down in Sister Bay, and he was afraid that if I did, he would have to report to work the next morning as the only employee at Ace Hardware who hadn't watched the moving of the medical center.

I tried to suggest that the reverse might be true — that he might be laughed at for being balmy enough to keep a vigil while the flimsy structure was trundled off its pilings, into the street, and up by way of highway 57 to its new location. However, that possibility struck him as being as intriguing as the first. He began to consider with relish the idea that he might be the *only* eyewitness and therefore be called upon to give a first-hand account.

Everett had what might be called a vested interest in the medical center. He had begun haunting the site since the project began, a matter of several months. Almost every night after the supper dishes were done — and sometimes he would coerce me by doing the dishes himself — he would take me for a ride into town so I could watch him and a nameless Swede, both of them built like retired construction superintendents — short-legged and barrel-chested — prowling around the timbers and the heavy machinery. With arms folded importantly across their chests, nodding judiciously, they would volunteer answers to the questions posed by the

Neither Everett nor the Swede knew anything of any substance concerning house moving, but they didn't let that stop them from conducting guided tours of the site and holding forth authoritatively about the technical aspects.

vacationing, polyester-pant-suited, blue-rinsed matrons who streamed out of the restaurant next door and who found the elevated edifice more fascinating than the goats on Al Johnson's sod roof.

Neither of these fellows, Everett nor the Swede, knew anything of any substance concerning house moving, but they didn't let that stop them from conducting guided tours of the site and holding forth authoritatively about the technical aspects and the finer points of the project. Nor were they at all reticent about explaining the reasons for the various setbacks and dogmatically naming the day and the hour the center would roll — something about which even the bona fide contractors weren't sure. I began to worry that if the powers that be didn't soon get on with the job, it would become an official tourist stop, and my Dutchman and the Swede would take to wearing hard hats and be tipped for their services. If they weren't arrested for their audacity.

Well, finally someone had gotten the act together, and here we were walking down Bay Shore Drive at one in the morning to witness the Big Event. Correction: I was walking. Everett was half-running, half-skipping, like a kid on his way to the circus, afraid it might begin without him. I was in no hurry. In fact, I felt a little foolish being out at such an hour, even if it was, as my spouse punned, "a medical emergency." It may have been a fortuitous night for moving a building, but it seemed to me a much better one for sleeping. I was there, I had to remind myself, for two reasons: one, to keep Everett out of harm's way; and two, to have something interesting to include in my letters to the children. It occurred to me that if I failed in the first of my objectives, I would have a much better chance of succeeding in the second.

It was my intention to take a back seat for the performance, to sit in the grass and on the fringe of the crowd. Everett's ambition was to sit in the cab of the truck that would winch the building along its route. We compromised. I selected a good spot on the lawn, about sixth row center, while he dashed off to make sure the expensive crew knew what it was about. I fully expected the sheriff to take him and his buddy, the Swede, who had also turned up for the launching, into protective custody; but there was a spirit of good-natured tolerance abroad, and they were allowed to kibitz at will.

From where I sat the whole affair had the aura of a small town concert under the stars, with people visiting back and forth between the inchings of the medical center. The Hatches were there and the Seaquists, the Caspersons and a host of folk we knew by face and not yet by name. All that the occasion lacked was a refreshment stand and the strains of Sousa or Strauss in the air. I gradually stopped worrying about my wandering husband and relaxed. It was pleasant indeed to sit in the grass and pass the time of night with neighbors, to exchange symptoms and recipes with the rest of the abandoned wives.

The event was hardly a cliff-hanger, but the crowds were there — as many teen-agers as oldsters. Who among us, I wondered, didn't have a story to tell of dislocated shoulders set straight, foreign objects removed from the eyes, vision tests and X rays and first aid administered in this building? So maybe our interest was not just idle curiosity, maybe it went deeper than that. But whatever it was that drew so many spectators, the actual moving of the center was so snail-like that the fascination soon began to pall. As the hours passed the old folks began to yawn and fade away, and soon Everett and I found ourselves surrounded by young people.

It was time to remind my husband that in three hours the building had advanced only a few feet from its site to the roadway, and there been turned so that it could be hitched to the truck that would complete the operation. It still had to be pulled past Johnny's Cottage Restaurant, past the Cove Gift Shop, and Jungwirth's Hardware and Bunda's Department Store. Then a sharp turn left and a further climb up the 57 hill and it would be home safe.

I informed Everett that I had lost my second wind and used up all my adrenalin. Even if the medical center broke loose at the top of the hill and plummeted wildly back down the main street and I wasn't there to see it, I couldn't care less. He admitted that he, too, was beginning to crumble around the edges, noted that the Swede was gone, that the Hatches were nowhere to be seen, and that he seemed to be the oldest survivor. It wasn't too difficult to convince him that he needed a nap before reporting to work in a few hours.

We walked slowly back to the car.

"Sorry I dragged you away," I apologized.

"Oh, that's all right," he answered, gaping, but gracious.

"Do *you* think they'll have any trouble getting it up the hill?" I asked.

He paused for a moment, a worried frown wrinkling his forehead, then resumed walking.

"Oh, sure, they'll be OK. We got it squared away and hooked up. They'll be able to manage it from there on without my help."

Everett, after reading my copy a year later, insists that he didn't say it that way.

"You should be more accurate," he warned me.

"What do you think I am?" I retorted. "A court reporter?"

There's no use trying to explain to my husband that I don't always write what he says he said, but what I *understand* him to have said, and sometimes there's a shade of difference between the two. And that difference is called poetic license.

"You ought to add," he chides, "that I am letting you tell this story — but only under protest."

So be it.

12

Friday Night at the Ferry Dock

MANY OF OUR CHICAGO ACQUAINTANCES who vacation in Door County drop in to see us from time to time for various reasons. There are the "auld lang syne" folk who come out of the purest of motives: to keep alive the old friendships. On the other hand, there are those whom Everett has labeled "Bad Weather Friends"; couples who have had the misfortune to be trapped here during a rare bout of nasty weather. Unable to go swimming, golfing, or fishing, and tired of being cooped up in their motel rooms, they will suddenly remember: "Hey, the Reichels live around here somewhere, don't they? Let's do 'em a favor and look 'em up."

There are other old buddies who tend to suspect my enthusiastic superlatives inscribed on the annual Christmas greetings about living snuggled up close to Mother Nature, and so they decide to check us out hoping to catch us in a lie so they can report back to the Chicago crowd that the Reichels are "alive, yes, but not living as well in their Eden as they would have you believe."

Whatever their motivation, I make it a point during the six-month tourist season to keep a supply of homemade Brownies and raspberry cream cheese pies in the freezer against unexpected and unannounced visits. Not that I hope to compete with the local patisseries; it is a maneuver meant to distract. I reckon that if our drop-ins enjoy my baking, they will be less likely to criticize the dust on the tabletops and the dog hairs on the upholstery.

Some of our guests repay our hospitality by bringing me up to date on the job I left behind me: the changes in personnel, the drop in morale, the proliferation of problems in the fringe area high school at which I had taught for twelve years. Those friends invariably say in parting, "You don't know how lucky you are to be out of it!" with much the same demeanor and expression they might exhibit if I were laid out in a funeral parlor and they had come to pay their last respects.

Other holiday visitors feel it their duty to let us know what we are missing by our renunciation of the world, and they hold forth on the latest plays, the concerts, the opera, the British re-runs on channel 11, the Folkfest at Navy Pier, Bonwit Teller's new store, *ad intimidatum;* and they usually get around to asking before they leave, "And just what do you do for excitement around here?"

Esther and Howard are of the latter breed. They were vacationing at Gordon Lodge last summer and stopped in on their way to a fish boil at The Viking. They were running a little early, they confessed, so they dropped in to have a little chat. Well, they deserved some credit for their candor, I decided, inviting them to leave the security of their silver Mercedes-Benz and hazard the less rarified air of our patio. They slid out of their chariot, dazzling in matching white slacks and Polynesian shirts. The old nature in me hoped our neighbors were taking note. We could use a few points in our favor, going around as we usually do, and as we were bedecked that afternoon, in what Everett calls our "fatigued

116

They slid out of their chariot, dazzling in their matching white slacks and Polynesian shirts. Everett and I were wearing our "fatigued outfits," paint-flecked, air-conditioned, frayed-bottomed slacks, demolition jersey tops.

outfits" — paint-flecked, air-conditioned, frayed-bottomed slacks and matching demolition jersey tops.

I couldn't help but notice that Esther's hair was newly bleached and coiffed. Mine, on the other hand, was done up in rollers, a mongrel set of green, yellow, and black rollers — for all the world to see, since I hadn't bothered to cover them with a scarf. Everett was not hurting that I could notice, what with Howard being bald as an egg and Everett long overdue at the barber's. I asked him to make our guests comfortable, hoping he'd remember to dust the lawn chairs first — the birds make free with them in our absence — and I went in to turban my head and make a pitcher of lemonade.

"We were here last night, but you weren't home," Howard explained when I returned with a tray of goodies. "We were on our way to the Hillside for a steak."

"Never home on Friday night," Everett said, passing the plate of pecan cookies.

"Date night, eh?" Howard asked cutely, winking at Esther.

"You might say that," I bristled, sensitive to the inference that we were too old for such shenanigans.

"Where do you go on a date up *here*?" Esther asked in a transparent attempt at appeasement, implying environment was our problem, not old age.

My mate and I exchanged glances and held our peace.

Howard broke in before the count of ten. "Whaddya do? Get all spiffied up and drive down to the Dairy Queen in Sturgeon Bay for a soda?"

"If I know Jocelyn," Esther teased, "their big Friday night date is shopping for groceries at the Red Owl."

I bit my tongue and freshened their lemonade. She knew me, all right, but I wasn't going to give her the satisfaction of letting her know she had scored. In the winter months, that shopping expedition was our big culminating activity for the week, with a Sara Lee cheesecake or a Deluxe Celeste pizza after the groceries were put away.

Howard was enjoying the sport. "Or do you spend the evening browsing through Nelson's Hardware in Bailey's Harbor?"

That coaxed a smile from us; we couldn't help ourselves. Nelson's is no ordinary hardware store; it is an experience — a bilevel labyrinth designed by a modern Daedulus. Any time we are at a loss for something to do, we take a quick inventory of the house and barn and find something we're out of or will be out of eventually and drive across the peninsula to Nelson's. If my concept of heaven is a Viennese pastry shop, then Everett's is a hardware store, and not just any Ace or True Value; it would have to be a Nelson's.

Esther refused a second helping of cookies. She nudged her husband and pointed to our bikes propped under the lean-to.

"Maybe they go out on the back roads and drag race," she suggested.

I decided the game had gone far enough; that it was time to parry some of the thrusts.

"None of the above," I denied, pushing a few picks back into the rollers and tightening my scarf, girding for battle as it were.

"Well, then?" Esther prompted.

I was about to give her the chamber of commerce cultural pitch: the art shows, the travelogues, the classes at the Clearing, the Peninsula music festival, when I was surprised by Everett's declaration.

"We go to the ferry dock at Gill's Rock."

Our company exchanged speculative glances; Everett and I swapped grins.

Howard waved a bee away from his half-filled glass. "And what do you do at the ferry dock?"

"We park," I answered, winking at my husband.

There was a short silence while they considered whether or not to pursue that line of questioning. It was Esther who decided to proceed — but cautiously.

"Why the ferry dock? Aren't there other places where you can be alone?"

"Oh, we don't go there to be alone," Everett informed her. "If we wanted to be alone, we'd stay home."

They helped themselves to some more pecan cookies while they digested that contribution.

Finally Howard asked, obviously humoring us, "What is your particular reason for preferring the ferry dock?"

"Well, that's where the ferry leaves from, don't you know?"

"If you're just going to see the ferry off, you don't have to wait until Friday night, do you?" Howard challenged, more than a little provoked at the way he was being fed information, piecemeal. "I mean, according to the schedule I happen to have here — " he pulled a timetable from his shirt pocket " — it leaves a total of seven times a day, seven times a week."

"We're talking about one particular sailing, Howard," I explained with exaggerated patience. "The eleven o'clock Friday night commuter special."

"What do they do? Send it off with a twenty-one-gun salute, or fireworks or something?"

"You gotta get there early," I continued. "You want to get a good parking place between the smoking sheds and the

120

marina. Right on the edge of the water so you don't have to get out of the car to watch the comings and goings.''

"How early? We were here last night at eight, and you were already gone. You said the ferry doesn't pull out until eleven — " Howard was beginning to sound hostile.

I continued with the leg-pulling. "As it was, we got off to a late start last night. I had both the lunch and supper dishes to wash and the picnic basket to pack — "

" — and she changed her outfit three or four times and took the curlers out of her hair," Everett embellished.

I intended to kick his shin, but that might have called attention to the bunion slit in my faded gym shoe. But pencil-slim Esther chose that moment to seize on the words "picnic basket," and I had to rise to my own defense.

"Well, it's a long evening, you see. That last ferry doesn't really leave at eleven — it's just supposed to. And besides, it isn't all food in that hamper. We throw in a couple of books and the binoculars and the camera and an extra sweater and a few dog biscuits for Poquito.''

"So what you do is sit there and read and snack and wait for the ferry?''

I was planning on introducing a little esthetica, like sea gulls performing overhead and the sunset over the bay and returning fishing charters blowing their horns triumphantly — I mean, what better place to just sit and wait for a ferry or whatever — but Everett remembered something else.

"The Cubs!" he exclaimed. "Don't forget the Cubs! On the nights they're playing out in Houston or on the West Coast we listen in on the car radio.''

"If the reception is good," I qualified.

Howard crossed and recrossed his legs, pinched the

121

knifepleat on his trousers, and asked quietly without looking up, "So you sit there and read or listen to the Cubs — aren't they eight or nine games out? — while waiting for the ferry?"

"They have a picnic lunch, too, Howard," Esther offered, by this time condescension thawing to pity. "Like we do at Ravinia."

I had seen an article on al fresco dining at Ravinia while leafing through a *House Beautiful* at the library, and I felt it necessary to contradict Esther, pity or no pity. It was not pate de foie gras, caviar, smoked pheasant, and champagne that we packed in our picnic lunch box.

"Not quite," I said. "Just HoHo's and Cokes."

"Sometimes Ruffles and root beer," Everett added. "Or peanut butter and jelly sandwiches and a thermos of milk."

"Well," Howard said heartily, starting to rise, "now we know what they do for excitement up here, don't we?"

"You have to understand," said Everett, refilling Howard's glass, ignoring his protestation, "that the suspense builds up gradually the nearer we get to eleven o'clock. Doesn't it, Jocelyn?"

"Oh, yes!" I nodded my head and shed a few more picks. "We keep count of the cars and campers that are lined up waiting for the ferry. You see, the ferry only carries about eighteen vehicles on the average —"

"And we wait to see how many will get left behind."

"I can see where that might be fun," Howard agreed. "Like watching someone get a pie in the face or slipping on a banana peel —"

"Now you've got the ticket," Everett chortled.

"Tell them about the stormy nights, dear," I urged.

"When the wind's out of the northeast —" he began.

122

"And the waves break over the dock —" I edged forward on my chair.

And the ferry can hardly pull alongside and let down the ramp —"

" —like the night they had to return to the island because they couldn't tie up?"

"And you know if the water's rough around the dock it's going to be murder out there on the open lake —"

"They don't call it 'Death's Door' for nothing —"

"And you wonder," Everett continued, a little winded at our enthusiastic antiphony, "how many are making the trip for the first time and don't know what to expect."

"And those who *do* know what to expect camouflage their anxiety by laughing and joking while the cars lurch up the heaving ramp and the ferry crew block the wheels —"

"Ever lost a ferry?" interjected Howard.

"No, we haven't," Everett replied, unable to hide a hint of disappointment in his tone. "But," he rallied, "the lake bottom is strewn with the wreckage of dozens of ships — sailing vessels —that didn't make it though the Door!"

"So once the ferry disappears around the bend, I suppose you are ready for home and bed."

"Oh, no," I protested. "Once it disappears around the bend we back out of our spot and head through the woods for Northport where Everett drives the car right out to the edge of the long pier —"

"And Jocelyn screams her head off, sure I'm going to drive off the edge in the dark!"

"And the winds rock our station wagon, and the waves inundate us —"

" —And every time the wipers clear the windshield we can see the bobbing lights of the ferry making her way

123

bravely toward Detroit Harbor. When she enters the harbor, *then* we go home.''

"If the ball game's over—"

"And the HoHo's are gone.''

Howard and Esther eventually drove off to their fish boil more than convinced that senility and solitude had combined to soften our brains.

"Do you think we did the right thing?" I asked Everett as we watched them turn onto the highway from our gravel road.

"Oh, yes," he responded firmly. "I think the 'Friday night at the ferry dock' routine is far more impressive than 'Watching Sydney Harris eat an omelet at the Country Kitchen'—"

"Even if I threw in 'Overhearing Norbert Blei tell the librarian he just made a sale to the *New Yorker*' incident?"

"In this case, even if," he reassured me.

"You know something?" I began, the demon in me surfacing. "The best part of it is that they'll never know whether or not we were telling the truth, will they?"

"It will torment them the rest of their lives," he agreed.

I returned to take up my household chores where I had left off, and Everett plugged in the car vacuum cleaner to probe the cracks and crevices for HoHo crumbs, potato chips, and loose change.

13

Cabin Fever

IT'S A WINTER AFFLICTION, cabin fever; every bit as real as bronchitis, frostbite, or Asian flu. Characterized by extreme irritability and restlessness, it results from boredom and is best treated by a change of scenery, activity, or company.

Everett and I were positive we were immune to the "virus"; after all, we are resourceful old-timers who have several hobbies going on simultaneously; we keep three library branches and the bookmobile busy supplying us with reading material; and most importantly, we are "winter people" who still, even in our dotage, get a thrill out of watching a blizzard (albeit from our living room window) and whose ecstasy mounts with the height of the accumulation.

In addition, Everett, although a septuagenarian, considers it effete to run a Toro up and down our paths; he wields a mean shovel instead, insisting on working alone. I share his enthusiasm for shoveling, but I am forced to seek a vicarious enjoyment. Between sections of Whittier's "Snowbound," I step to the window to cheer him on, or caution him to slow down, or invite him in for a frosted doughnut and cuppa to share the "Shut in from the world without . . ." feeling that Whittier relished, and so do we.

No, people of our disposition and life-style could not possibly be susceptible to the claustrophobic breakdown associated with cabin fever. No way. We not only *think snow,* we importunately pray for it. It wasn't the sunshine lushness of summer that caused us to fall in love with Door County. On the contrary, we became enamored on a bleak and blustery January weekend when we motored up from snowless Chicago ostensibly to see the snowmobile races. Our real reason for the trip north was that it had been years since we had experienced the exhilarating combination of clean snow and fresh air, and we hoped to ventilate our lungs and carmine our cheeks. Arriving too late for the races, we rented our own snowmobile, borrowed a pair of oil-stained coveralls for me from the owner of the Standard station in Ephraim and set out to find out what these new-fangled machines were all about.

We zoomed across the fog-shrouded, frozen bay toward what we were told was the Peninsula Park bluff. We made it by dead reckoning, and for an hour we varoomed and bounced over the hilly fairways of the public golf course at the park; took photos of each other at the ''controls'' to send to our grandchildren, and then, finally deafened by the din and sickened by the noxious fumes, we returned our rented vehicle fully persuaded that that was not the way to celebrate winter, an opinion we hold to this day.

We did not give up on that weekend, however. Nothing daunted, we spent the remainder of our time happily floundering through waist-high drifts and flirting with frostbite on a long hike along the frozen shore. We sipped hot chocolate in a rustic restaurant, and at night, from the comfort of our motel room, watched a magenta sunset on a polar bay. Mayhap we could resist the summer blandishments of Door

126

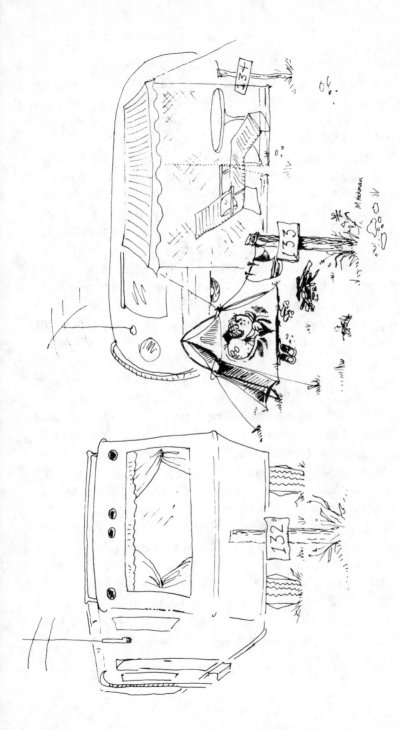

We tried the Florida cure . . . the economy package.

country, but in her winter habiliments we found she was a femme fatale. We were head over heels after one snowy weekend, and we are still captivated, more than eight years later, by her hiemal charms. That's why it was absolutely absurd to think that we could develop cabin fever.

Another factor that precluded our falling victim to the blahs-bug was that we had added skiing to our list of winter accomplishments — which already included shoveling, reading, mini-crafts, and Scrabble — Nordic skiing, a sport that took us into the wilderness areas quietly, harmoniously, and, after a good bit of practice on my part, effortlessly. We geared up and stepped out, rationalizing the modest expenditure as another weapon with which to combat boredom, the culture medium of the cabin fever bacillus. We found skiing was much more than a preventative — it became an obsession. Once having been on skis, there was no holding us in Chicago over the weekends. We turned our courtship with Door into a permanent relationship by buying a mobile home and setting it down in the heart of the "thumb." At that point our city apartment became our pied-à-terre, and our home in the woods our raison d'être! On our skies we had entered into the treasures of the snow! Cabin fever, indeed!

I think those who contract the disease must be completely insensitive to nature at her loveliest. "Always beautiful Sister Bay" was the favorite expression of a former local pastor as he opened his Sunday morning worship service. "Welcome to always beautiful Sister Bay!" I know he felt that way about the whole of northern Door, no matter the season or weather, but I'm sure he would agree it is particularly and breathtakingly so when it is counterpaned in drifted white; when snow devils whip along frozen bays; when hoarfrost silvers whole forests; when the elements are in command

128

and the sunshine patriots have fled to their retreats in Sarasota, Phoenix, Brownsville, and other points south and west. Then is the time the countryside is most dramatically and fantastically captivating. A case of cabin fever in a fairyland of sparkling delight? Not if one can get out to enjoy it, and we do.

Cabin fever has a history of attacking on a weekend. We ward it off by keeping on the move. "Want to go for a ride?" Everett will ask on a Sunday afternoon in January. Poquito will stop her excited gyrations long enough to have her knitted coat zipped tight, and I will sling the camera and the binoculars over my arm and off we go.

No matter what car we drive, sporty little Nova hatchback or its successor, the Chevy wagon, my husband treats it as an all-terrain vehicle. Icy back roads, snow-blocked lanes add zest to his outing. I don't especially appreciate the zest; sufficient for me is the infinite variety of the scenery — a variety enhanced by the blanket of snow. Our ride may take us over to Ephraim, the historic Moravian village that claims the most paintable sunset on Green Bay waters during the summer tourist season. Ephraim in winter, because of that same western bay, has another distinction, the highest snow drifts on the peninsula. The highway through town takes on the appearance of a mountain pass as the winter progresses, and eventually the view of the bay is blocked by a wall of snow.

We park our car, find an opening in the barricade, walk out onto the ice as far as we dare, and turn around to view the village, a Christmas-card sketch in pen and ink of spires against a gray sky, frosted evergreens marching up the hillsides, and white cottages limned among the trees, barely visible. Returning to our car we watch the ice skaters near the shore and turn our binoculars on the snowmobiles a mile out and the brightly colored ice boats and the activity around the fishing shacks. Everyone celebrating life — Winter life. No cabin fever in Ephraim.

There are a lot of people who can stave off a case of cabin fever over a plate of pancakes and lingonberries at Al Johnson's Swedish Restaurant in Sister Bay. On a Sunday afternoon in January, we can dawdle over our meal — no long line of hungry patrons waiting for our table; and the diners across from us are most likely neighbors, and we exchange gossip across the aisles.

A weekend afternoon is a good time to drive out to the tip of the peninsula, north through Ellison Bay and on to Gill's Rock, no longer the port of call for the Washington Island ferry. Its harbor is ice-locked, the wharves, fishing sheds, pilings, all sheathed in tons of ice — a photographer's dream. But it cannot compare with what awaits us at Cave Point. South of Jacksonport, several miles down a wooded lane, lies a glittering fairyland of sculptured ice and crystal branches, painfully dazzling in the sunlight; an admission-free display of God's artistry. No man-made sculpture can duplicate what the wind and the waves create: shimmering stalactites and stalagmites, great white thrones and rhinestoned bowers, winter grasses preserved under glass and strewn with brilliants. Surely a snow queen holds court here! There is nothing in the summer season that can compare, we say for the hundredth time, with the peninsula's winter carnival.

Cabin fever? No need. Not when there's companionship aplenty — a brotherhood of survivors such as we have. As the "snow birds" head south, those of us who remain close ranks, and the singing at the Senior Citizens' dinners, led by

130

our resident Welshman, Don Stott, increases in gusto. Bethel and First Baptist hold monthly potlucks to fend off the blues. The Clearing is open for square dancing and art classes, weaving and writing, chair caning and chorusing, French lessons and gourmet cookery, and a lot of other legitimate excuses for getting out of the house.

Boredom in the winter? Nonsense! There are birds to be fed: grosbeaks, woodpeckers, chickadees, and crows. There are the books to be read — and if the town libraries don't have them, the Bookmobile will — and they are delivered conveniently close to our doorstep by Bob Heilman, a librarian who truly knows his merchandise.

It is impossible to come down with cabin fever if one hits the ski trails five or six times a week. We usually hie over to Newport for our skiing, and we're likely to run into Phil Austin and wife, taking a morning off from his easel. Or septuagenarian Ralph Erickson, who could write a book on "The Joys of Skiing." Or madcap Al, getting in his twenty miles per diem. On the other hand, there is senior citizen Eric Swanson who keeps a mens sana in corpore sano, not on skis, but on skates. He carries his ice skates to the weekday dinners and exercises on the rink next to the Ellison Bay School, working up an appetite for smoked pork chops and applesauce. We envy, but we dare not emulate him, lest we break a leg and end our skiing fun.

No, when one considers all the offerings of our playground peninsula, there seemed to be no reason at all why we should fall victim to cabin fever. We weren't confined to a one-room shanty with only each other and the dog to contemplate. Our mobile home is a large one; our respective dens are at opposite ends of a fourteen by seventy rectangle, and when the doors are closed, we are, for all practical

131

purposes, completely isolated from each other. In addition, Everett has his "doghouse," a barn workshop equipped with a small space heater. He has his errands and the barber shop and his semi-weekly breakfasts with his cronies in town. I have my Underwood, my volume of Diacrostics, and my French language tapes.

We should be blissfully content. And we were, our first winter. It was our second winter that became the winter of our discontent. Suddenly even the Biltmore Mansion could not have held the two of us, and it was an effort to be civil to each other, let alone the dog. Everett could not part his hair to please me, and I couldn't poach an egg to his satisfaction. Books lost their savor, and we were fed up with crooning "Down By the Old Mill Stream" and "If You Were the Only Boy/Girl in the World" at the pre-dinner senior citizen sing-alongs. I burst into tears if the mailman was five minutes late or if the toaster failed to pop. I began to throw things, soft things like pillows and pot holders. When I advanced to slippers, Everett hid the knives and the scissors. The doctor prescribed a change in medication, but my doldrums only intensified.

Oh, we knew what was wrong, but we were reluctant to admit it. We were suffering from a satiety of winter. A bitter, record-breaking, month-long siege of arctic weather had kept us off our skis and confined us to the house for days on end. We had come down with cabin fever *in extremis*.

It is just too bad that human beings cannot go into hibernation. If only we could have eaten a few hefty meals, turned down the thermostat, crawled into bed and pulled the covers over our heads, setting the alarm for spring, we might not have made the mistake of attempting the Florida cure. But we were devastated and desperate. Florida seemed to work for at least half of our neighbors; maybe we should try it.

Our budget wouldn't allow us to go first class, so we took the opposite alternative — we went native. We picked up a tent at Mac's Sport Shop in Sturgeon Bay, bought a pair of thermal mattresses at the Omnibus in Fish Creek, and then went home and loaded our station wagon to the roof and beyond with all the accoutrements necessary for roughing it at a tender age.

As Everett was cinching the last rope on our luggage carrier, I asked him if he had noticed that our cabin fever had begun to dissipate the minute we had started making plans for the trip. While he was securing the bikes on the rack at the rear, I pursued the irony and suggested we could even stay home and read travel folders and road maps until spring, thereby saving ourselves a lot of grief and cash.

"Are you crazy?" he asked, waving his arm at the overburdened car. "We have already passed the point of no return."

We spent three weeks, and all of our traveler's checks, in the Southland, nursing sinuses badly irritated by pulp mill pollution and bumper to bumper fumes. We discovered at our first picnic table that we had beaten the mosquitoes but not the gnats. We couldn't help but notice several days into the tour that all KOA facilities are located on the shoulders of six-lane super highways, or, as was the case in Sarasota, at the end of the major runway of the international airport. Furthermore, no matter how carefully we selected our sites in the campgrounds, choosing them for privacy and elbow room, we would awaken in the morning to find ourselves sandwiched between twenty-four-foot Airstreams and colos-

133

sal motor homes that had backed in during the night.

Our moment of truth came when we found ourselves kayoed by the combination of heat and concrete sidewalks in Silver Springs. It was all we could do to make it from bench to bench, let alone visit all the exhibits. We knew then, alas, that we would have to scrap our plans for Disney World and Busch Gardens. And it was when we were taking our third free glass-bottomed boat ride — and only the presence of alligators prevented us from dangling our aching feet over the side — that we heard a pair of tourists gleefully discussing a blizzard that had swept Wisconsin the day before. We asked them to repeat the facts as they had heard them on their radio that morning.

"Makes you really appreciate the Florida sunshine, doesn't it?" one of them asked.

I'm glad he didn't expect an answer. We were all of a sudden too homesick to give one. We completed our vacation with dispatch and hurried home, convinced the cure had been worse than the disease.

Now it is winter again. The dead of January. Did we take any precautions this year to fend off a second attack of cabin fever? You bet we did! I am typing this on a kitchen table in a Quebecois farmhouse, 1400 miles northeast of Door County, approximately 480 kilometers north of Montreal. Everett has just gone to collect the eggs from a flock of thirty Rhode Island Reds. When he finishes that chore and is through slopping the two half-grown pigs that share the hen house, he will have to go down into the cellar and split a few more logs for our airtight.

I have not been exactly idle myself; it is 8 A.M. and I have made the beds, done up the dishes, chalked up another victory over the antique washing machine and hung up the clothes in the uninsulated attic where they will freeze-dry before I bring them down to the warm kitchen and drape them over the furniture to complete their drying overnight. I have a box of Petit Buerre cookies at my elbow, an addiction I will have to kick when I return to the States, and a Coke.

I look out the window and see snow-blanketed, wind-swept hills, pine and cedar forests, and the ski trails, half-obliterated, that we made yesterday afternoon. It is much like a Door County landscape, only rougher, higher, windier. It is wilderness country, ten miles from town; and Rang Cinq, our gravel road buried underneath a foot of ice and snow, ends a few hundred yards beyond our house. The temperature this morning was −38°F, and it will probably reach a high of −10°F before the sun sinks down behind the hill to our west. What they say about the cold up here is true — you really don't feel it. Everett knows that for a fact. He discovered last week that he had three frost-bitten toes, but he can't remember when or where he got them.

What are we doing in this kind of predicament at our age and in our condition? Suffice it to say that we were prevailed upon, offered a chance to be useful, by our daughter and son-in-law, Wycliffe missionaries in Quebec. That appealed to us. But the real clincher was our daughter's promise that we would be able to escape the threat of cabin fever by the challenge of a new environment. In record time, we got Betsy and ourselves outfitted for the arctic, closed our home for the winter, and now here we are six weeks into our noble experiment.

Have we come down with *fievre de cabane?* Well, not yet. During the day we laugh at the idea, but at night when the fifty-mph winds howl around the eaves and our transistor emits nothing but rapid-fire French, and the nonfunctioning TV sits dumbly in its corner, and we vainly search our shelves for some volume we haven't already read twice, we are not so confident.

I am afraid that it is waiting, this *maladie,* to pounce on us at the precise moment we fit the last section of blue sky into our 2000-piece jigsaw puzzle. I recall the delaying tactics of one Penelope, wife of Odysseus, who was off fighting the Trojan War among other things. When eager suitors insisted that her husband must be dead and pressed her for her hand, she promised she would give them an answer as soon as she had finished weaving an intricate shroud for her father-in-law. Clever Penelope unraveled each night what she had woven during the day, thus keeping the suitors at bay. It may be a strategy worth trying with our jigsaw puzzle — we hear tell the winters up here around Lac St. Jean can linger until the Fourth of July.

14

The All We Got Away From

"SORRY," Paul Hulbert commiserated. "No *Trib* today."

I picked up my bag of groceries from the counter, pulling a sad face, thereby earning a joshing from Paul as he opened the non-automated door of the Beach Road Market.

"I thought you city folks came up here to get away from all that crime and violence. What do you want the paper for?"

City folks, indeed! I grinned weakly and made for the car where Poquito was enthusiastically barking me aboard, drowning out any clever retort I might have made. Not that I had one ready; my bons mots are pretty slow in surfacing, usually occurring to me when the interested party has long gone, and after a good deal of cogitating out loud and to myself. *Esprit d'escalier,* the French call it—the repartee that comes to mind too late, when one is halfway down the stairs after the adieus have been said and the hosts have locked the door and are on their way to bed.

So I cogitated, taking the long way home so that I could mull over the question: "What do you want the paper for?"—a question I inferred to mean: "Haven't you weaned yourself completely from city living?" But if we had, then why had I almost responded with a "Touché!" to the grocer's challenge?

Two years had gone by since we handed over the keys to our Chicago apartment to our landlord and pointed our laden station wagon north. Were we now, after all this time, becoming a little homesick for the bright lights, traffic jams, and rapid transiting? Was rusticity beginning to sour? Were we unconsciously longing to return to the "all we had got away from?" Our friends had warned us we would rue the day. Were they right? And was our daily dependency on the *Chicago Tribune* evidence of their astuteness?

Certainly by this time we had been living on the Door "thumb" long enough to make an honest assessment. Surely we had enough seasons under the belt so that we could deal objectively with their warnings: "You'll be sorry!" "You're making a mistake!" "It won't last!" All predictions voiced by most of our friends when we had announced our plan to flee and burn our bridges behind us. It might have strengthened our case somewhat if we had been able to claim the move was based on doctor's orders; but even my physician, who had been treating me for chronic hypertension, took a negative view. He was unmoved when I insisted that Door County was a land of cloudless skies and encouraging words.

"It will be the best thing in the world for me," I argued. "I will be living 'north of the tension line.' " (I borrowed a familiar quote from the Chamber of Commerce — the "tension line" being an imaginary line separating the rat race from the fugitives and lying somewhere in the middle of the Sturgeon Bay bridge.)

"You will succumb to ennui in six months," was his prognostication.

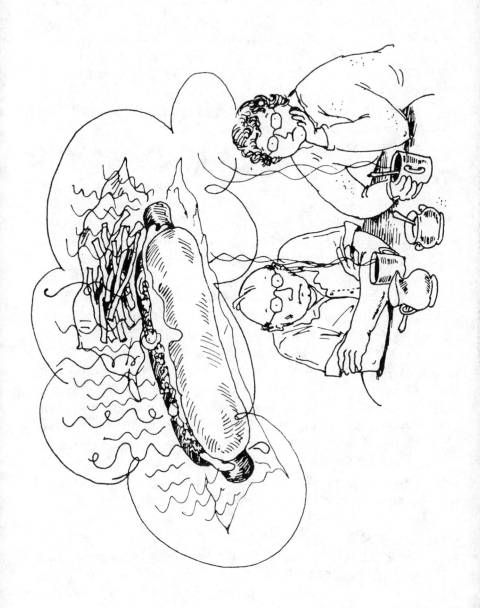

Our doctor and our friends may have had misgivings, but we had no qualms whatsoever about turning our escape hatch into our permanent address. Our decision had not been based on personal whim but on many months of prayer, and we were confident this was God's will for our life. We laughed at all the dire predictions, convinced that they were, on the whole, well-intentioned, but showed little confidence in our resourcefulness along with a lack of understanding of the situation. After all, we were not going into this premature retirement "cold." For five years we had been sampling the good life north of Sturgeon Bay. In addition to long summer vacations and Christmas fortnights (fringe benefits of the teaching profession) there were the weekends — several years of them — when my husband would meet me at the school door on Friday afternoons and within five minutes we would be on the ramp to the north-bound Edens at Irving and Keeler, leaving behind our high-tension jobs and enjoying the gradual decompression process as we increased the distance between ourselves and the city. My fists would begin to unclench at the Des Plaines toll booth; my sinuses would clear thirty miles north of Milwaukee; and driving along the Manitowoc lake shore I would abandon the niggling worries about whether Everett had remembered to lock the doors, turn off the lights, shut the windows, etc. By the time we were sitting down to steaming bowls of Chicken Booyah in the cozy A&M in Two Rivers we were both hanging loose and behaving like a couple of kids on a holiday from school! Invariably and every weekend!

Conversely and naturally, the return trip on Sunday was a gloomy one. Our spirits would plummet as we approached Chicago and the responsibilities that awaited us there. I was especially affected by those manic-depressive weekends because although Everett had already retired from his thirty-year career with the Railway Express, I still had a long way to go before I could retire without penalty.

There came a time when the therapeutic weekend escapes were no longer enough; a medically prescribed leave of absence did not make my heart grow fonder; the years until retirement stretched before me like an eternity. I was in truth, "burned out" as a teacher; and so, with Everett at my elbow, I wrote my Dear John letter to the school board.

Then, packing our favorite bed and my husband's battered La-Z-Boy, distributing the rest of our furniture among the children and the Salvation Army, we surrendered our apartment and left the city in which I had been born, schooled, married, and had reared my family. We drove off with a remnant of our worldly possessions, a couple of pounds of corned beef from Link's Delicatessen, a stockpile of rye bread from Beil's Bakery, and a lifetime of memories. I did not do a Lot's wife; I was too eager for the adventure that lay ahead.

Now, after two springs, two summers, one glorious fall and a record-breaking winter, how were we doing? Had we proved our compatability with boondockian climate and culture? I looked around me for a handy metaphor and found one in what passes as a garden in our neck of the woods. Seven years earlier when this retirement home had been only a weekend hideaway, we had brought two plants with us from Chicago, picking them up at a nursery on the outskirts of the city with no assurance that they would be able to withstand the rigorous climate of northeastern Wisconsin, not to mention surviving the inept handling of us amateur gardeners. One, a mock orange shrub, was about

141

four feet tall; the other was an infant clematis, about two feet in height.

"We'll probably be sorry." I told Everett as I sat on a boulder nearby and watched him "dig" a hole for the philadelphus in a shelf of rock at the corner of our mobile home.

"I already am!" he grunted between swings of the pick-axe. He thrust the bush into the hole lined with rock chips and sandy fill, threw in a few shovels of potting soil, watered it well, and expressed the hope it would last the summer. Now, after seven summers, it is ten feet tall and five feet wide, held to those dimensions by my clumsy pruning. Each June the number of fragrant white blossoms increases, and for the rest of the season it is a luxuriant privacy hedge.

Our clematis, too, is thriving. Everett has had to reinforce and enlarge the supporting trellis twice. From late August through early November, its huge purple flowers, cascading from vines twelve feet tall, advertise its contentment with its surroundings. Oh, there were setbacks along the way. The first year out, we almost killed the clematis by having it too close to the reflective surface of the house; and we spend a small fortune on malathion each year so that our mock-orange will not end up completely defoliated by a leaf-curling spider. But they are blossoming where they are — proof positive that their transplant was successful.

"All right," I concede to my conscience. "At least they're doing a lot better than we expected."

And I suppose that's what our drop-in friends from Chicago say about us: "They're doing better than we expected." One or two of them, the doctor included, might add, "But then we didn't expect very much!"

How, indeed, were we doing?

I parked the car in front of our small barn, set Poquito down on the snow-covered path, and carried the groceries into the house.

Everett rose to greet me and to help unpack the paper sacks.

I stopped him with a question. "Everett, are we beginning to miss the 'all we got away from?' "

He poked around among the groceries again before answering. "Is that your way of telling me the *Tribune* didn't come?"

"It's going to spoil our whole day, isn't it?" I asked in mock dismay.

"Well, maybe get it off to a less than perfect start," he agreed.

Groceries tucked away, we sat there over our unnecessary and illegal morning snack, sadly bereft.

"You know, Thoreau said newspapers are unnecessary, a foolish waste of time," I reminded Everett.

His reply was a derisive snort.

I persisted. "He said that if you read about one fire or one murder or one death of a mad dog, you've read about them all. You don't have to keep on reading about them over and over again."

Everett held his peace and helped himself to a second doughnut, a powdered sugar one that snowed all over the front of his brown flannel shirt.

"Maybe we ought to cancel our standing order," I suggested. "You know, cut the silver cord, as it were."

"It's OK with me," he barked. "I can do without it."

My heart skipped and then resumed an anxious tattoo. I hadn't expected him to take me up on the suggestion. I didn't know if I could survive too many days without Mab-

143

ley and Greene and Beck, without Abby and Dr. Timothy Johnson, Andy Rooney, and let's face it — without the obituaries!

"Yep," he said, getting up from the table and taking his dishes to the sink. "I can do without it; but I don't think Poquito could. You know how wild she gets when I head for the chair with the newspaper in my hand; can't wait to settle down with me while I read it."

He was pulling my leg. Poquito wouldn't care if he sat down with the telephone directory — just so long as he made room for her.

I returned to the question after clearing away the crumbs and rinsing the dishes. "Do you think we are getting homesick for the big city?"

"Only one way to answer that. Do you want to go back?"

I shuddered. I have a recurring dream, a nightmare in which the two of us are driving south on I-94, heading back to Chicago. It's a nightmare from which I awaken in a cold sweat, clutching my pillow in a stranglehold.

"Contemplate the alternative," Everett added, repeating the phrase that we both use when we find ourselves in the middle of a Door County doldrum. The alternative — life in a neat, well-maintained, middle-class Chicago neighborhood — was well worth contemplating. Within a five-year period we had had two bicycles stolen — along with other valuables — from our yard and basement; two new tires lifted from our car parked in front of our house; two car break-ins; lunch hour marijuana parties in a bungalow across the alley; rapes and muggings within short blocks of our home; a maiming of one of my students; and the murders of three close acquaintances — separate, shocking, violent incidents. We double-locked our doors against thieves

144

and left our storm windows on in the summer against air that was heavy with industrial fumes.

No, I had no desire to return. But maybe Everett was being less than candid. I tried to wheedle a confession from him.

"Be honest now. Surely, there are some things you miss—"

"If you must know, there are," he admitted. "For one thing, I miss seeing the Cubs on TV—"

"Oh, yes," I agreed. "Twelve months of Bart Starr and the Packers is a bit too much!"

"How about you? What do you miss most?"

I should, I suppose, have said the museums, the Art Institute, the Chicago Symphony, but we were baring our souls, and I felt I had to match my husband's candor.

"Well, the Cubs first," I conceded. "But a close second would be hot dogs!"

Everett choked—was it a sob or a doughnut remnant?

"You mean—"

"Uh-huh, Vienna hot dogs from the stand at Addison and Kedzie!"

"Or Irving and Central—"

"Or almost anywhere in Chicago!" I groaned, cutting him off. The memory was almost too painful to endure. Since leaving the city we have sampled hot dogs from Algoma to Green Bay to Gill's Rock trying to find a reasonable facsimile of a Chicago hot dog and have met with total failure. Our oldest daughter, 1,400 miles away in Sept Iles, Quebec, wakes up in the middle of the night with a craving for the tough-skinned Vienna dog, tucked into a steaming bun and oozing mustard, catsup, piccalilli and onions; plus a paper twist of greasy, salted, and thoroughly browned fries

145

on the side. Well, so do I, so do I.

Our son in Mississippi, married and in his thirties, admits that he still experiences withdrawal pangs after ten years away from Chicago and its infamous hot dogs.

Everett and I used to send out for this delicacy when there was something to celebrate and when there was nothing to celebrate. When I was dieting and when I wasn't. And, oh, the thousand and one nights when we went out for a couple of hot dogs, a tamale or two, and throw in an extra wiener without a bun for the Chihuahua!

For a few minutes Everett and I sat meditating silently on the joys of gorging on hot dogs al fresco, until he remembered, "Field's — you forgot Marshall Field & Company!"

Oh, no, I hadn't. Forget Field's, that emporium of earthly delights? If it weren't for the catalogs they sent me periodically, Field's would be at the top of my most missed list.

Well, we had known we would have to leave some good things behind along with the bad, and we had been prepared to make the sacrifice. But the daily newspaper and the importance it would have in our northern retreat had never entered our minds. How could it? How could we have anticipated that we would come down with a serious case of contempt bred by familiarity? That we would get so used to sandy beaches and spectacular vistas, quiet woods and cherry blossoms and apple orchards, and life in a four seasons playground that we would find our Eden becoming humdrum? And that the result would be the perverse delight we take in our coffee and *Trib* break each day when we read and gasp at the horrors happening in the old home town: the violence, the corruption in high places, crime in the streets, insubordination in the schools. And our initial

146

shock is followed by a delicious and smug sense of deliverance. Sad to say, we are titillated for the day by our vicarious exposure to the "all we left behind."

Yes, the doctor was right when he prognosticated that boredom would get us in the end — but it did that in Chicago as well. And if we are bored at times, it is no one's fault but our own for not organizing our days and our weeks more productively.

There were those who said we would soon become disenchanted. They were right, too. Columnist Sydney Harris wrote about an irony of life that applies here: once you can afford something, so can everyone else. We hadn't realized when we made our break with urban living that we were in the forefront of an invasion army — a wave of humanity looking for the same peace-among-the-pines that we were seeking — so that the wilderness which drew us here in the first place is disappearing.

So, have we come to rue the day? Most everybody said we would. The answer is no. The air is still sweet, freshened as it blows across the lake and across our peninsula from almost any direction; the back roads are still quiet and lined with pleasant pastoral scenes; the dear hearts and gentle people have not left.

But there *is* a feeling akin to regret that surfaces occasionally during the tourist season. It struck me one Friday night last summer when Everett and I were loading our shopping cart at Krist's, keeping an eye out for specials and trying to keep our discount coupons in alphabetical order, a grim task. The store was crowded with summer people buying charcoal and potato chips and cases of pop, the usual picnic fare. They were laughing, carefree vacationers, hyper with the same exuberance, the same abandonment to joy we used to feel on our senior sneaks, before we made the permanent move and got away from it all. Before we became accustomed to Paradise.

I pulled Everett aside between the laundry supplies and the pet food. "You know what I wish?" I asked him wistfully. "I wish we could be tourists again, just for tonight!"

15

There's Nothing to Worry About!

IT IS EVERETT'S FAULT that I am a fuss-budget. Early in our marriage I decided that I would have to do the worrying. One of us had to, after all, and since it was not in my spouse's nature to be anxious for anything, I had to assume the responsibility. His favorite expression in the face of any impending crisis was then, is now, and forever shall be: "There's nothing to worry about!"

In the first months of our marriage, I took that to mean that I should relax, that he would take care of the situation and have it well in hand and under control in no time at all. Such was not the case; my hubby was as vincible as the next mortal, with feet of clay, and although highly skilled around the house (he knows twenty-five ways to prepare eggs, can stifle a leaking faucet, and can rewire a faulty switch) there is a limit to his genius. When he confronts a challenge for which he does not have the expertise or the tools, he resorts to "There's nothing to worry about!" That is the precise moment when I begin to show concern. Or make contingency plans. Or map my strategy.

I don't think I'd mind nearly as much if Everett didn't get such a bang out of situations that send me up the wall. And although he has tried to calm my anxious fears through a

great many crises, he lacks the necessary qualification —
empathy. What frightens *me,* titillates *him.* I am scared to
death on roller coasters and ferris wheels; he roars with
laughter and opts for seconds. I weep and wail when Betsy
throws a spark plug; he revels in an afternoon of kibitzing at
the mechanic's elbow. Those sorts of things.

I can remember — will I ever be able to forget? — when I
had gone into labor with our second baby, and Everett was
unable to beg, borrow, or commandeer a taxi. We had to be
transported twenty miles across town in a paddy wagon.
"There's nothing to worry about!" he kept reassuring me as
we bounced around in the rear of the Black Maria, while he,
holding onto one-year-old Martha and me at the same time,
was unable to conceal his sheer glee at the madcap race
through the Loop, down the Outer Drive, over to Hyde Park
Boulevard and the Lying-In Hospital. When he thought of
it, when he paused in his enjoyment of the caper from time
to time to notice my pale face and look of anguish, he would
hasten to placate with "Now, now, there's nothing to worry
about!"

Small comfort. A lot he knew. There was plenty to worry
about. I selected the most horrible eventuality, and bracing
myself around a sharp turn shivered at the horrible vision of
giving birth in the police wagon and reading about it in the
morning *Tribune!* Well, it didn't happen. I almost wish it
had. It would have been worth the "I told you so!" Instead,
Everett had the satisfaction of saying when our son Tom
arrived an hour later in the delivery room, "See, there was
nothing to worry about!"

"There's nothing to worry about," Everett said several
summers ago when the transmission went out on our tour
bus as we were climbing up the Pike's Peak highway. The

What frightens me,
titillates him!

perspiring driver finally managed to back the rear of the bus into a retaining wall to stop our frightening descent, and while I pushed and elbowed my way past the slower evacuees, Everett was happily grinning, snapping pictures, and chortling, "Take your time; there's nothing to worry about!"

It was on another trip that our widely divergent approaches to life's emergencies became even more apparent. We were flying the Apache line from Las Vegas to Kingman, Arizona — through a wild sandstorm. There was only one other passenger on the small craft; he was evidently a veteran commuter and had taken the precaution of tanking up before boarding. Our plane bobbed like a ping-pong ball between the rugged mountains. Everett, high on excitement, and the other passenger, high on alcohol, laughed and joked through it all. I took my cue from the pilots, whose collars were wilting and whose faces were grim. I closed my eyes and prayed. Everett kept turning around to urge me to relax, to unclench my fists, to open my eyes and look around.

"You may never come this way again," he said. "Take a good look! It's sensational! Come on, there's nothing to worry about!" And then he added the old bromide which I myself have frequently used during rough flying weather: "These pilots want to get home, too, you know!"

We did make an uneventful, if turbulent, landing in Kingman — but a week later the same plane, on that same trip, crashed into the side of a mountain during a sandstorm, and everyone aboard was killed. "See," I told Everett, illogically, but triumphantly, "there *was* something to worry about!"

There was a time when I thought early retirement would

152

restore me to a more reasonable state of mind, but the truth of the matter is that I have developed a low anxiety threshhold. If I am not in the middle of a crisis, I am expecting one by nightfall, or around the next turn in the road. Even in Door County. Even in this beauteous thumb of land "north of the tension line," I am thrown by dilemmas. Everett learned that last fall when he suggested a long, curative hike through the woods after noticing my barometer was falling.

We drove out to Newport for our trek, left the beaten path after a few minutes to see if we could locate our old ski trail, and in no time we were lost. "Lost?" scoffs Everett, whenever I tell the story. "Not on your life! Just disorientated." Whatever, we didn't know where we were or how we had gotten there. To make matters worse, it was a raw day; fog was rolling in off the lake; it was late afternoon, soon to become dark, and we were clad in thin jackets. The woods we were in were what I call "rotten woods," with fallen trees blocking us on all sides; mosquitoes above and snakes presumably below, and I held a shivering Chihuahua in my arms. I panicked. I dashed back and forth and in circles. I babbled.

It made no difference to me that the wilderness in which we were groping was a mere 2,000 acres. Lost is lost is lost. It wasn't until my cool, unflappable Dutchman grabbed hold of me on my third hysterical rush toward a break in the underbrush and said firmly, "There's nothing to worry about!" that I was finally restored to rational behavior. A smart slap across the face could not have brought me to my senses any more quickly than did the exasperation aroused by the familiarity of that maxim. A few minutes later, mortified into silence, I shamefacedly followed my husband down the path we had been seeking. Everett had shinnied a few feet up an old tamarack and found our path, all of five or six yards away.

Even in retirement, even in never-never land, the only stimuli I need to push the panic button are a slight change in the hum of the refrigerator, or the acrid odor of burning wires as we drive down the highway in our overworked wagon, or the ringing of the phone after ten o'clock in the evening. Or just let the faucet chatter and vibrate, and inside of a minute I have, in my creative worrying, torn apart the sink, dug up the lawn all the way to the pump house, and depleted my checkbook balance to pay the plumber. Or let the furnace develop what our furnace man calls "a delayed spark," the resulting roar and rumble causing my dishes to rattle on the shelves, and I begin to collect my irreplace- ables, and try to read the directions on our extinguisher, worry about whether our insurance is paid to date, position myself and the dog near the door, and wonder if it is serious enough to phone the fire department, or the furnace man, or Everett, who's at work at the golf course, and who will probably tell me, "There's nothing to worry about!"

And then the air works its way through the water line, and the furnace settles down, and I collapse into the nearest chair and berate myself. Mea culpa! What am I, a Christian, doing bogged down in Ecclesiastes? Overcome by the van- ities and the vexations of this world? Down in the mouth and uptight and under a cloud! Almost eager to prove the prediction that my golden years will be tarnished, and that I will take no pleasure in them!

Eons ago, when I was seventeen and a new convert, I had an appointment with the pastor of the church I hoped to join. It was the church at which I had gone forward to accept the Lord; a beautiful edifice, built to resemble an English

154

countryside chapel, with a formal, oak-beamed interior that encouraged reverence. While I was speaking with the pastor, the Welsh choir director and song leader stepped in to see about the music for the next week.

"By the way, Ivor," the pastor said, "I think we ought to be a bit more careful about the kinds of choruses we sing at the evening service. That one you introduced last week, that 'Cheer Up, Ye Saints of God!' was a bit rowdy for the setting, don't you agree?"

The music director acquiesced, but not very happily; and as he turned to leave, I heard his muttered protest: "But it's a good song! A true song!"

A good song, it is; and true, and we sang it for years, Everett and I, and we taught it to our children.

> Cheer up, ye saints of God!
> *There's nothing to worry about!*
> Nothing to make you feel afraid,
> Nothing to make you doubt.
> Remember, Jesus never fails;
> So why not trust Him and shout!
> You'll be sorry you worried at all tomorrow morning!

We sang it *en famille* at devotions; we shouted it earsplittingly in our loaded carry-all, traveling cross-country; we crooned it in close harmony around campfires and at youth meetings; and we let it ring out unabashedly in Scottish dialect at evening service in a church that was not concerned about marring its ambience.

It was from that chorus that Everett borrowed his line. When he tells me "There's nothing to worry about," we both know where he is coming from. It is a gentle nudge reminding me of—forgive the syntax—where I am at. I need fre-

155

quent nudging. One daughter, writing to me out of a deeper experience than I have ever known, reassures me: "Nothing is out of God's control. He cares for you with perfect wisdom and the greatest of love. Remember David's testimony 'Yet in my heart Thou hast put more happiness than they enjoyed when there was corn and wine in plenty. Now I will lie down in peace, and sleep; for Thou alone, O Lord, makest me unafraid.' "

"Come to the land north of the tension line!" the chamber of commerce invites, and the invitation has the same dynamic impact on the harried urbanite as a Rapala on a Coho. And it is just as deceptive—for there is no such land. There is no Shangri La, no adobe hacienda, no grass shack on a Pacific atoll, no wilderness cabin to which one can flee, where one can lead a care-free existence.

No, there is no place. But there *is* a Person. And He said:

> Come unto me,
>   all ye that labour
>   and are heavy laden,
>   and I will give you rest.
>
> Take my yoke upon you,
>   and learn of me;
>   for I am meek and lowly in heart:
>   and ye shall find rest unto your souls.*

There's nothing to worry about, at all, or ever again, for those who love God, for those who accept Christ's invitation! And isn't that the perfect Retirement we all are seeking?

*Matthew 11:28.